The Architecture of
Perry Dean Rogers & Partners

COLOR
&
CONTEXT

MICHAEL J. CROSBIE

ROCKPORT
PUBLISHERS

Rockport Publishers, Inc.
Rockport, Massachusetts

First published in the United States of America by:
Rockport Publishers, Inc.
146 Granite Street
Rockport, Massachusetts 01966
Telephone: (508) 546-9590
Fax: (508) 546-7141

Distributed to the book trade and art trade in the U.S. by:
AIA Press
1735 New York Avenue NW
Washington, DC 20006
(800) 365-ARCH

Other Distribution by:
Rockport Publishers, Inc.
Rockport, Massachusetts 01966

ISBN 1-56496-138-9

10 9 8 7 6 5 4 3 2 1

Art Direction/Cover Design: *Laura P. Herrmann*
Design: *Connexus Visual Communication/Lucas H. Guerra and Oscar Riera Ojeda,*
Laura P. Herrmann
Layout: *Connexus Visual Communication/Lucas H. Guerra and Oscar Riera Ojeda,*
Cover Photo: *United States Embassy, Amman, Jordan*
Richard Mandelkorn
Back Cover Photos: *(top) United States Embassy, Amman, Jordan*
Richard Mandelkorn
(bottom left) Villa Amanda, Westport, MA
Steve Rosenthal
(bottom right) Science Center at Wellesley College, Wellesley, MA
Richard Mandelkorn

Printed in China

TABLE OF CONTENTS

_A_CKNOWLEDGMENTS

Many people contributed to the completion of this book. Special thanks to the partners and staff at Perry Dean Rogers & Partners, especially Charles Rogers and Liz Porzio, for their tireless responses to requests for material and information; to the people at Rockport Publishers, especially Rosalie Grattaroti and Shawna Mullen, for their help in producing the book; and to the various photographers and their assistants for their timely responses to requests for photographs.

For Brigit Rose, who arrived in the middle of this one.

*I*NTRODUCTION

Old and venerable architecture firms tend to reach their zenith through the talents of their founding partners, and then limp to obscurity in the hands of less-capable heirs of the practice. Perry Dean Rogers & Partners is a sterling exception to this rule. One of the oldest practices in Boston, the firm started in 1923 as Perry Shaw & Hepburn, and excelled in traditional American design, making its mark with historic preservation and restoration projects. During the Depression (1929-1939), while other firms failed, Perry Shaw & Hepburn was commisioned as the architect for the reconstruction of Colonial Williamsburg, Virginia. The firm went on to build a solid reputation as campus architects for Brown University and other elite clients.

Today, none of the founders remain, but Perry Dean Rogers & Partners continues at the forefront of college architecture and institutional building design. It has maintained its position through the addition of new design talent to the firm over the years. The firm occupies the top floor of the century-old Grain Exchange building in the heart of Boston, not far from Faneuil Hall. The studios under the building's cone-shaped roof inhabit a space filled with intricate trusswork, reminding one of the expressive structure found in many of the firm's latest projects. While Perry Dean Rogers & Partners exhibits the same attention to detail and care of execution that marked the firm's work more than a half-century ago, its approach to design remains fresh and inventive, engaging and compelling. The result is architecture that is responsive to its users and the context, and that is distinguished by a bold use of color inside and out.

*T*HE ROLE OF CONTEXT

Because many of its buildings are part of the larger whole of a college campus or an urban site, Perry Dean Rogers & Partners is sensitive to the issue of context. For less talented architects, "contextual" designs often become anemic replicas of what is already there, pale reflections weak in both detail and execution. In contrast, Perry Dean Rogers & Partners never simply copies the context. The existing architecture—its materials, scale, massing, orientation, detailing, color, use of light, and its role in the greater fabric of a place—is simply a point of departure, a palette from which to draw upon in the design of a new building. The new buildings add another element of richness to the mix; not a weak copy, but an architecture with its own unique presence that is a good neighbor as well.

One of the best examples of this inventive response to context is the firm's design for the Seeley G. Mudd Chemistry Building at Vassar College. The new building completes the fourth side of an implied quadrangle created by other science buildings on campus. It is roughly the same width and height as the building it faces across the quad, and its materials echo those used in the older buildings: brick walls, limestone belts, repetitive windows, white trim. While the older buildings have sloped copper roofs that have weathered to a bright green patina, the new building's roof is flat and contains a top story. Its sheet metal is painted green to match the copper roofs of the older buildings. Here is a palette of contemporary materials, rendered in a contemporary way, that nonetheless respects the older buildings nearby.

Sometimes an architectural context does not exist, and it is the architect's role to invent one, or imagine what one might have been, or recall one's own memories in a "wished for" context. An example of this is found in the Villa Amanda, which occupies four acres of a riverside meadow in southern Massachusetts. The site had been part of a shipyard in the mid-18th Century, and Villa Amanda recalls the widow's walks commonly found on the houses of sea captains. But this house is also a notation on the architect's love of Palladian architecture, rendered in wood in the naive fashion that one might expect from an 18th century Yankee carpenter-builder.

At the opposite end of the spectrum of a refined, "wished for" architectural context are the gritty mill buildings of early New England industrial cities such as Lowell, Lynn, and Worcester. Here the context is embraced equally, as seen in the Marshall's Wharf II project in Lynn where a condominium industrial building takes its cues from the city's long, brick mill buildings. Glass block, an unglamorous material associated with factories and other industrial structures, here adds sparkle to the brick facades.

THE CHARACTER OF COLOR

Lest one believe that Perry Dean Rogers & Partners has mastered an architectural response only to buildings close to Boston, consider their design for the U.S. Embassy in Amman, Jordan. Faced with an architectural context that is far from that of New England, the architects relied on a sensitivity to what is already there, studying the methods of construction and use of ornament native to the region. Here, materials are virtually restricted to native stone. But from this limited palette a richness is derived from the combination and juxtaposition of smooth and articulated surfaces, with ground and rough-cut stone. The context of intense natural light, of surfaces grazed with the desert sun, is much of what this design is all about. Present too are stylized interpretations of native ornament, in the diamond-shaped window grilles and intensely orange doors—geometry and hues common to the products of Bedouin weavers. At the embassy there is a seamless integration of context and color, one reinforcing the other.

A trademark of the firm's work is the use of saturated color to enliven spaces and to contrast them. A large portion of the firm's work is for colleges and libraries, buildings that will be in use for many years, and where people will spend long periods indoors, often at night. On the practical side, color helps alleviate fatigue and keeps the eye stimulated. Interiors with intense colors washed by natural light are a constant play of contrasts, marking the time of day, offering different shades and hues from hour to hour. Colors can give a space depth, as may best be seen at the Shore Country Day School, where in the compressed space of a corridor subtle differences in color lend it a dimension impossible to achieve with white walls. When viewed under constantly shifting light, colors sculpt the space, creating a collage of shadow and hue.

Color is also used to make a building intelligible on an architectural level, to explain how the structure works with the mechanical systems, the fenestration, and the elements of enclosure. The cylinder of space created by the spiral staircases at the Science Center Expansion at Wellesley College—a jumble of materials and surfaces— is made intelligible through color. Pipes, ducts, and electrical conduits are articulated with different colors, as is the window sash, the edge of the ceiling, the railing, and the wall surface. Thus the viewer has a more coherent understanding of the building's constituent parts, and how they work together.

At times color can create the context itself, helping us to understand the building's function. This is best demonstrated by the exterior of the USPS General Mail Facility in North Reading, Massachusetts—a large warehouse clad with economical metal panels. Here color not only articulates the cladding's elements of corrugated surface, ribs, and bolts, it also suggests the facility's contents by rendering the building as a gigantic mailbox.

Perry Dean Rogers & Partners' manipulation of color and context makes its work satisfying to an audience of architects. But its buildings are not designed solely for that audience. The architecture wears well and is appreciated by those who use it day-in and day-out, long after the paint is dry and the pretty pictures have been taken. One of the highest forms of praise for an architect's work is to be called back again by clients, as this firm has been. It is the long-term test of the work, appraised by those who live with it, that affirms the architecture of Perry Dean Rogers & Partners.

Michael J. Crosbie
Essex, Connecticut

TOP ROW (left): *The weblike interior of the firm's attic studio. Photo: Richard Mandelkorn*

(center): *Local materials, with ornament and color inspired by native crafts, distinguish the U.S. Embassy in Amman, Jordan. Photo: Richard Mandelkorn*

(right): *The templelike Villa Amanda responds to a "wished for" context. Photo: Steve Rosenthal*

CENTER ROW (left): *A space at Hamilton College's Student Activities Village shows intricate trusswork. Photo: Richard Mandelkorn*

(right): *At Wellesley's Science Center, color distinguishes the interior's various elements. Photo: Richard Mandelkorn*

BOTTOM ROW (left): *At the Shore Country Day School, various shades and hues of color give the space depth. Photo: Steve Rosenthal*

(center): *The brick exterior of Marshall's Wharf acknowledges its gritty context of industrial architecture. Photo: Edward Jacoby*

(right): *Curved metal cladding at a postal facility, rendered in bright colors, suggests that the building is a giant mailbox. Photo: Steve Rosenthal*

SCIENCE CENTER
AND SCIENCE LIBRARY

The 240,000-square-foot Science Center at Wellesley College houses laboratories, a library, classrooms, lecture halls, and faculty and administrative offices for eleven science disciplines. This 150,000-square-foot addition is connected to Sage Hall, a 19th-Century Collegiate Gothic building, by a 60-foot-high atrium, covering space that was formerly the older building's exterior courtyard. Bridges tie the building together on three levels, and lend the interior a Piranesian atmosphere. The exterior has a Gothic rationality. Its concrete column, beam, and slab structure is infilled with glass, while vent stacks for the laboratories are celebrated as contemporary finials.

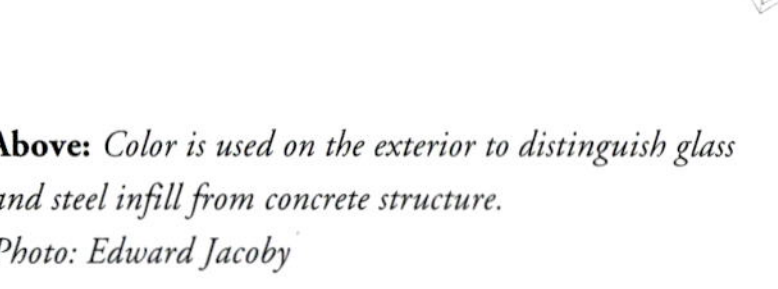

Located on the ground floor of the Center, the science library brings together collections formerly scattered among five departmental libraries. With colorful, flexible stack space organized in a central location, both interdisciplinary and specialized research is accommodated. Study carrels line the outside wall of both the main floor and mezzanine. Additional programmatic areas include lounges, group study rooms, seminar rooms, and audio-visual rooms.

The center is characterized by its flexibility and by a unique "systems" approach applied to all elements of construction, from the structural and mechanical aspects of the building to the architect-designed laboratory furniture. Open planning of two 60,000-square-foot laboratory floors allows the easy reconfiguration of laboratory space to suit the introduction of new equipment or additional space demands. The flexible laboratory furniture system designed for the project is now in commercial production; its adaptability allows any lab to be modified, reversed, or converted from "wet" to "dry" without tools in under an hour. Throughout the lab, color is used to code mechanical, electrical, and plumbing equipment.

Wellesley College experienced an unpredictable increase in science course enrollments after the completion of the Science Center and Science Library. The college was so pleased with this building that they commissioned the architects to design a major addition to it.

Above: *Color is used on the exterior to distinguish glass and steel infill from concrete structure.*
Photo: Edward Jacoby

Right: *A typical stairtower bay meets the ground on concrete columns, allowing vegetation to grow beneath it.*
Photo: Edward Jacoby

Above: *A view from the upper-level bridge of the focus
area and the brick elevation of Sage Hall.
Photo: Edward Jacoby*

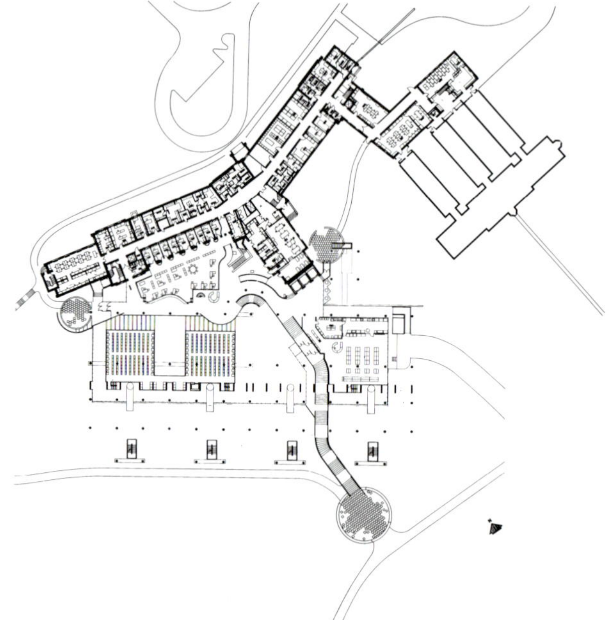

Above: *Bright colors are used within the library to distinguish it from the gray concrete structure.*
Photo: Edward Jacoby

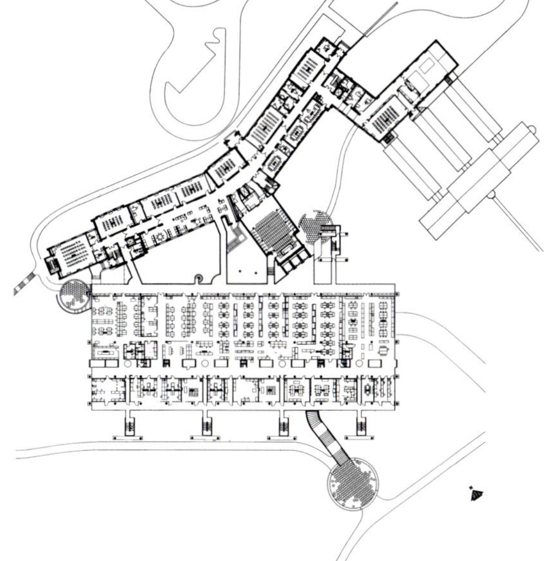

Above: *The focus area, as it sits between the brick walls of Sage Hall and the concrete structure of the addition, has a Piranesian quality.*
Photo: Edward Jacoby

Left: *Lab counters in bright colors are fully demountable and can be moved within an hour.*
Photo: Edward Jacoby

Below: *High windows illuminate the sculptural quality of the exposed structure.*
Photo: Eduard Jacoby

Opposite Page: *The multi-story area is the center of the addition and allows access to the various function spaces.*
Photo: Edward Jacoby

SCIENCE CENTER EXPANSION

Dramatic growth in student enrollment and rapid changes in science technology impelled Wellesley College to expand the 1977 Science Center, which earlier had united all the science disciplines in one complex, promoting the cross pollination of ideas and allowing each science discipline to share the Science Library, lecture halls, classrooms, and special equipment.

The expansion adds 41,000 square feet of state-of-the-art classrooms, physics and optics labs, a computer science lecture room, computer carrels for academic and computer science, additional faculty research areas and offices, and microbiology, chemistry, and geology laboratories.

The introduction of new technologies in the field of pure science and also in science education had the greatest impact on the form of the expansion. The importance of the computer to both the sciences and the greater Wellesley College community inspired spaces designed to be easily accessible to all. The open and inviting character of the 1977 addition set a strong precedent for the design of primary public spaces.

The expansion is a diagonal infill of courtyard spaces between the 1922 Sage Hall and the 1977 addition. The 60-foot-high atrium, filled with natural light, houses an academic computing area of separate work stations with bright orange canopies, creating a computer village. The addition makes extensive use of glass block for interior and exterior accents. All mechanical, electrical, plumbing, and fire protection piping, ducts, and conduits are exposed to view, individually identifiable by their bold, saturated hues. The contemporary, economical exterior is in the spirit of the earlier addition, with its Galvalume pre-formed, metal wall panels.

The expansion incorporates the best features of both its predecessors; a combination of private offices, controlled classrooms, flexible laboratories, and colorful public spaces.

Above: *The exterior of the expansion as it joins the Science Center addition in the background.*
Photo: Richard Mandelkorn

Right: *Orange canopies throughout the computer village mark separate work stations.*
Photo: Richard Mandelkorn

FIRST FLOOR PLAN

1. *Academic Computing*
2. *Laser Laboratory*
3. *Faculty Offices*
4. *Computer Science Seminar*
5. *Library*

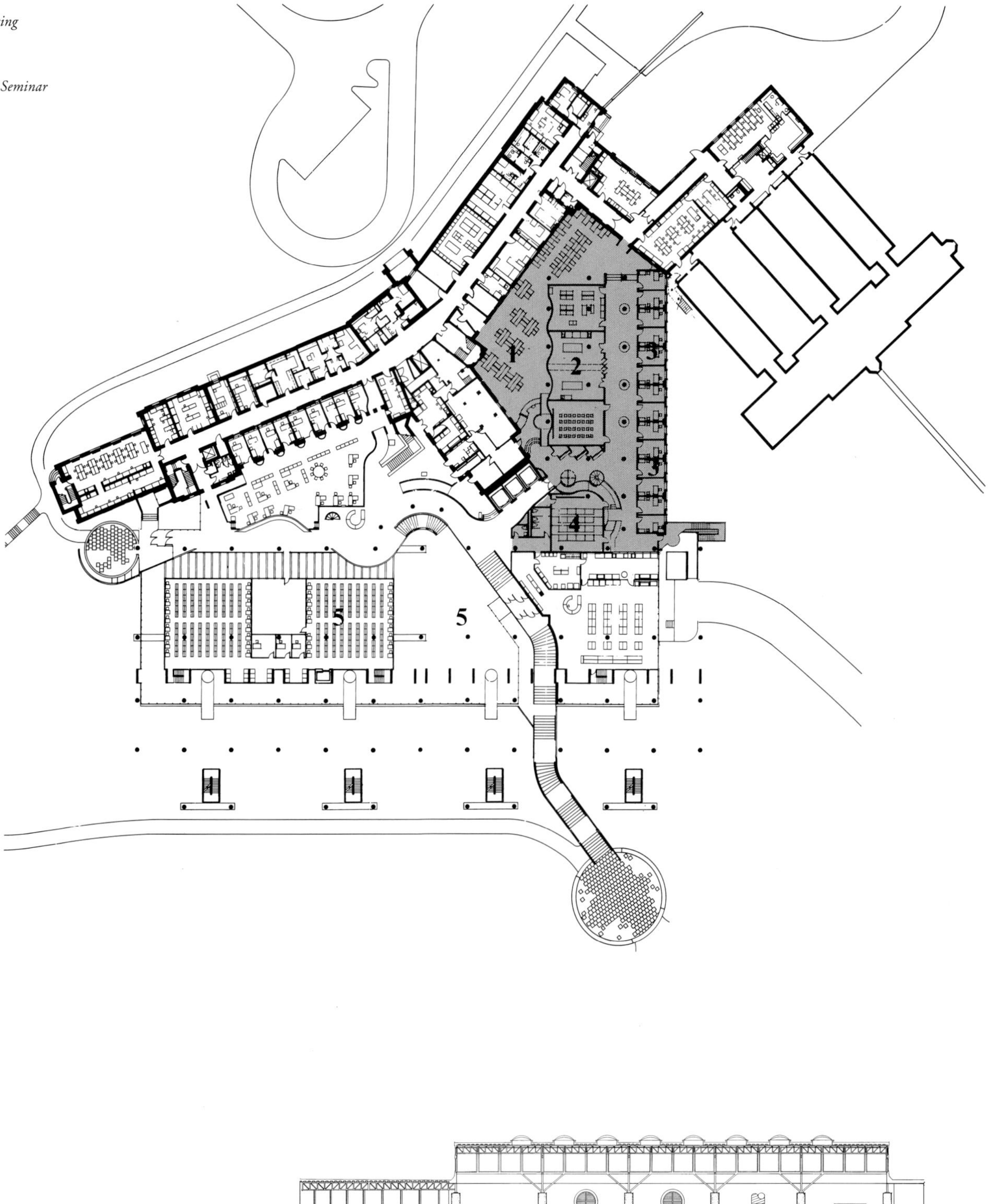

Left: *Canopies contribute to a strong, colorful theme on the ground floor of the atrium.*
Photo: Richard Mandelkorn

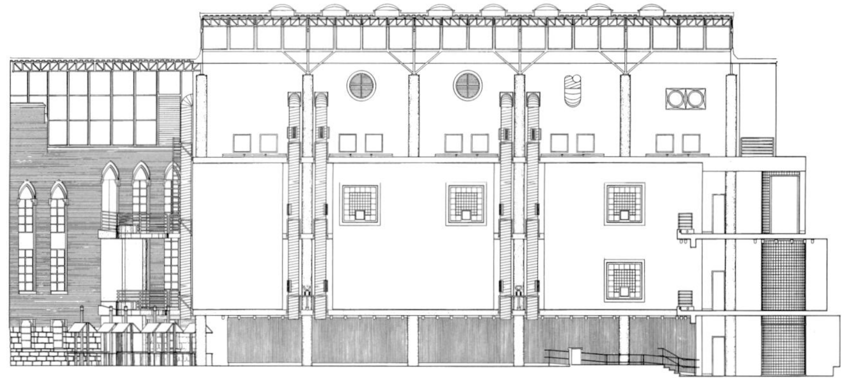

SECTION

Above: *The view straight up from the spiral staircase presents a collage of color and light.*
Photo: Richard Mandelkorn

Right: *Colors are used throughout the interior to distinguish lighting fixtures and utility elements such as ducts and pipes.*
Photo: Richard Mandelkorn

Below: *Glass-block-enclosed spiral stairs offer quick access between lab floors.*
Photo: Richard Mandelkorn

Opposite Page: *Skylights, structure, and exhaust ducts create a surreal roofscape.*
Photo: Richard Mandelkorn

SOUTH POSTAL ANNEX
REHABILITATION

The original postal facility occupied a 1934 industrial warehouse located on the Fort Point Channel and attached to a 1960s addition. This rehab added a new pedestrian passage from South Station and a new main entrance facing Fort Point Channel. Also added were a new mechanical system to maximize the efficiency and minimize operating costs, and a new skin to wrap the building.

An articulated pedestrian connector located along the north end of the first floor of the building provides a direct, enclosed, and recognizable circulation link between the west entrance (South Station), the post office lobby, and the main entrance on the east side of the building.

An automatic control system, incorporating a central console in the engineer's office, allows for control and monitoring of all mechanical equipment and electrical demand. Both air intake and distribution ductwork are made economical by locating the low-velocity air handling units on the existing mezzanine levels and adjacent to the east facade of each floor.

The primary ductwork distribution spine runs north-south on each floor. Secondary ductwork distribution branches off perpendicularly from the primary spine and parallel to the structural grid in an ordered system that visually relates, along with the lighting system, to the repetitive structural bays. The expression of the ductwork on the facade creates a strong sense of the building as an efficient, powerful machine.

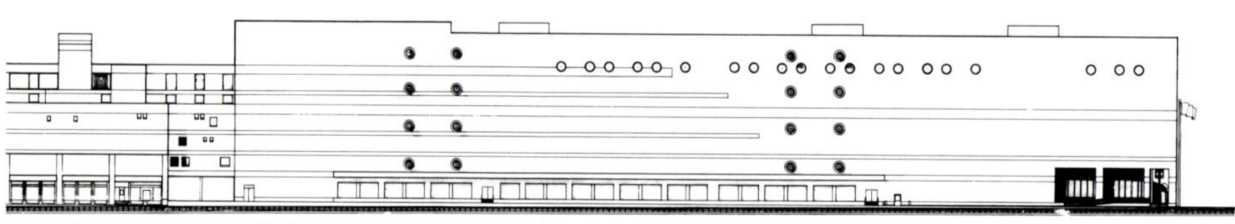

EAST ELEVATION

Above: *An upgraded mechanical system is vigorously expressed on the building's facade.*
Photo: Peter Vanderwarker

Right: *Horizontal stripes on the facade express the building's linear nature and swift postal delivery.*
Photo: Peter Vanderwarker

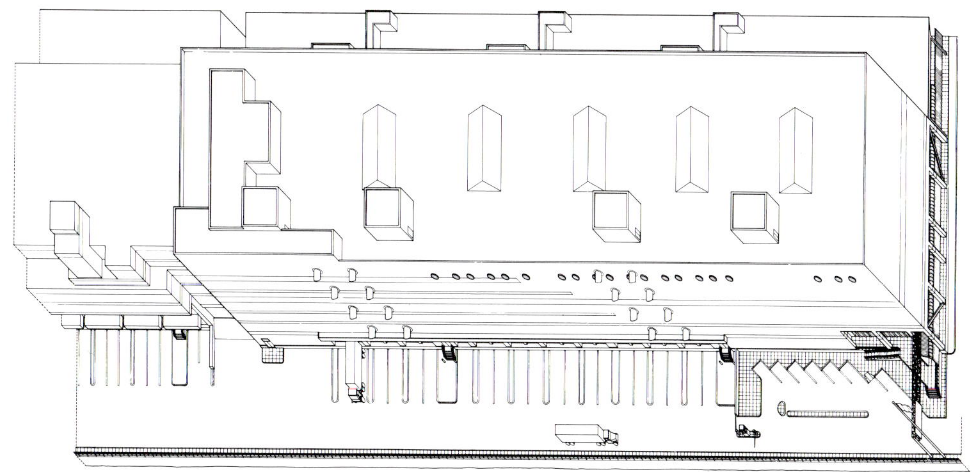

AXONOMETRIC

YMCA OF GREATER WORCESTER

Originally built in 1917, this community athletic facility had been haphazardly expanded and modified during more than 65 years of use and abuse. The site had deteriorated and become densely packed, and was unattractive to the local downtown business community. Committed to the downtown location, civic leaders decided to renovate the original facility to a state-of-the-art recreational, social, and fitness center.

The dense site was cleared to provide a foreground to the original gymnasium/pool facility. A new wing, which houses offices, entry lobby, a control desk, and a double-height atrium, was introduced between the street and the original structure. The entry axis, which is terminated by the atrium, forms a

"seam" between the old and new and separates the public and private areas of the building. The form of the seam is a small-scale replica of the original gym roof profile skewed from the primary grid to address the direction of approach. Color, pattern, and form playfully mimic elements in the original structure.

Given the budgetary restrictions of a service organization, the design aesthetic could not depend on expensive objects or specialty products for its appeal. Instead, common industrial-type products were used in a creative way to achieve an exciting design. High-pressure light fixtures used as chandeliers, bright colors, and glass block combine well to create a lively interior and exterior expression.

The design has become a landmark example of building reuse and has provided a growth stimulus and an urban amenity to a rundown section of the city of Worcester.

Above: *The tall gabled entry element acts as a "seam" between old and new and separates public and private areas.*
Photo: Richard Mandelkorn

Opposite Page: (top) *A detail from the mezzanine level above the atrium reveals complementary bright colors used throughout interior.*
Photo: Richard Mandelkorn
(center) *The double-height atrium, astride the lobby, gives the building a civic scale.*
Photo: Richard Mandelkorn
(bottom) *The pool area features a mezzanine level for observation of swim meets.*
Photo: Richard Mandelkorn

Overleaf Photo: Richard Mandelkorn

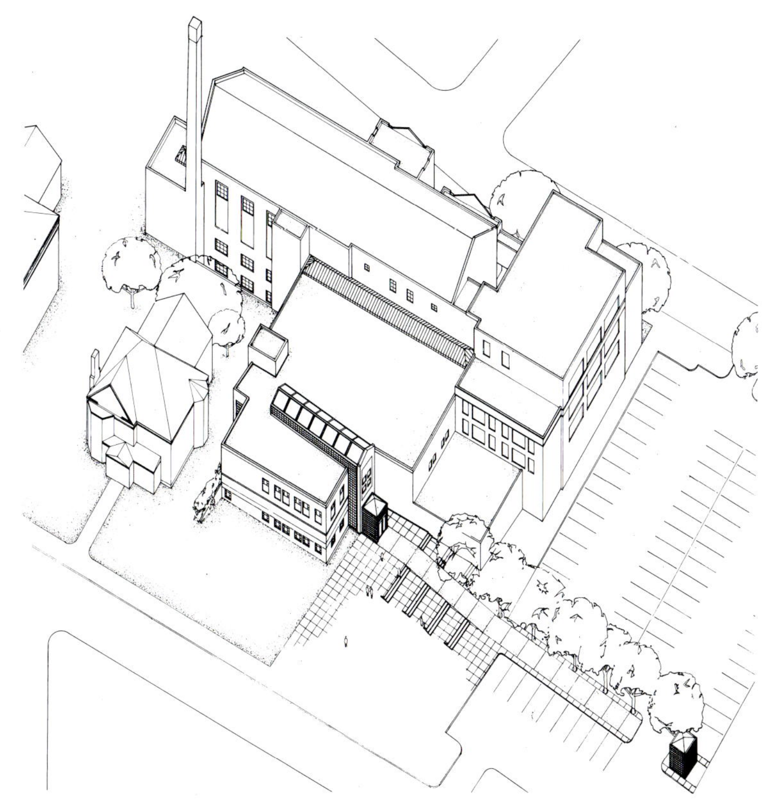

AXONOMETRIC

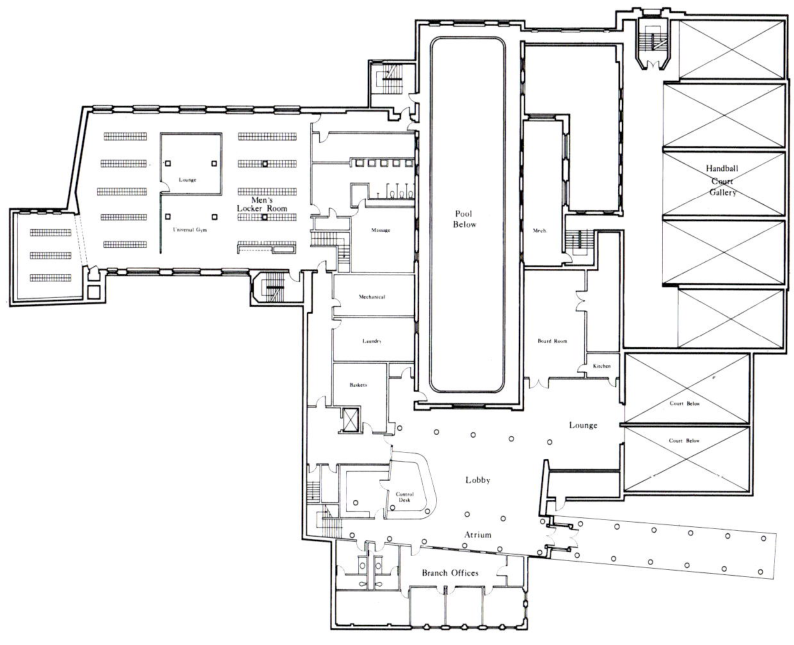

SECOND LEVEL / ENTRY

MARSHALL'S WHARF II

This wharf project is located in a Boston suburb, once a busy industrial city, which is now on the threshold of an urban renaissance. Nearly a century ago, the city housed brick clad industrial buildings in many of the areas that are now affected by urban blight.

In the spirit of that bygone era and in an effort to revitalize the downtown area, city officials commissioned a light industrial building to replace a structure of similar function that was destroyed by fire. Conceived as a condominium for commercial use, the building has open bays with large loft areas that are appropriate for subdivision both horizontally and vertically—to suit a variety of light manufacturing and office uses. With a central spine flooded by daylight and

with decorative use of brick, glass block, and granite, the building recalls the industrial architectural vocabulary of the past.

The surface of the masonry structure, treated with brick, glass block, and granite, refers to the construction motifs and materials of early 20th Century industrial architecture. The building evokes the context of a now destroyed industrial city and seeks to maintain that history in a new context.

Glass block was chosen not only for security: Lynn has a history replete with the use of technological innovations, including tool, die-making, and textile production. Glass block represents technology created in the modern industrial climate, but used in a fashion that makes a gesture appropriate to a former time. It permits light to enter and define interior spaces, and provides a glittering facade that embraces Lynn's present and past.

Above: *The Marshall's Wharf II entry is recessed to give it prominence and to create shadows on the facade.*
Photo: Edward Jacoby

Right: *The exterior employs materials commonly found in Lynn's industrial architecture, such as steel, glass block, and brick.*
Photo: Edward Jacoby

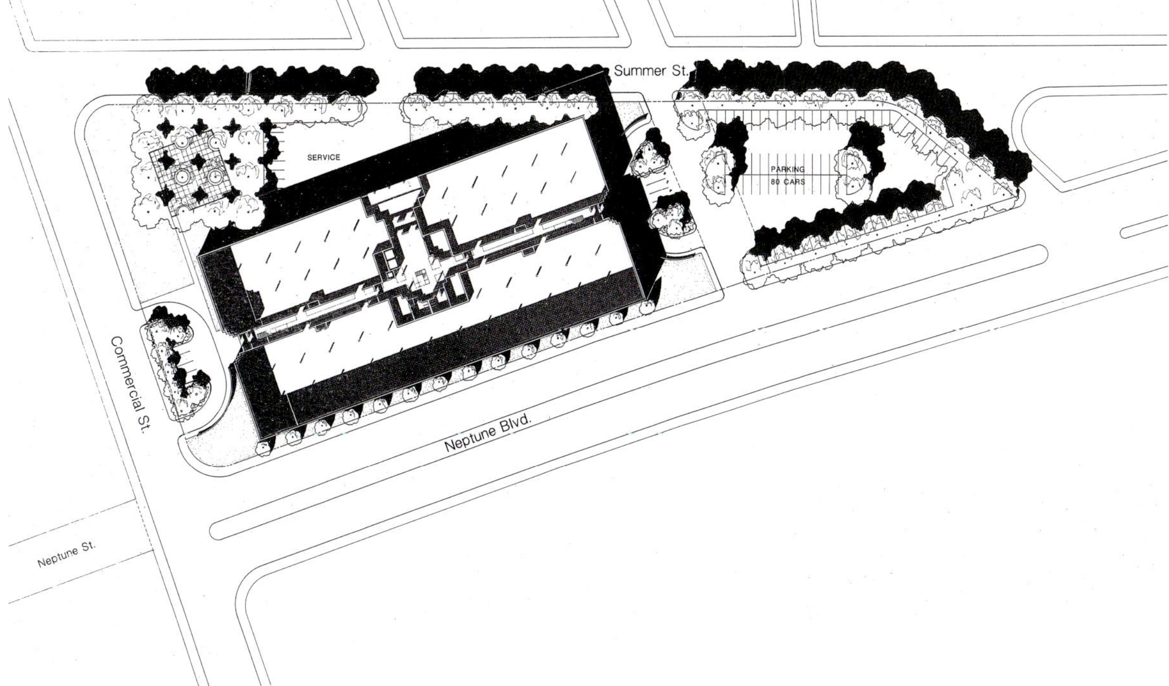

Summer St.
SERVICE
PARKING
80 CARS
Commercial St.
Neptune Blvd.
Neptune St.

Above: *Viewed from the lower level, the central stair creates a kaleidoscope of steel and light.*
Photo: Edward Jacoby

Below: *In the staircase, simple elements of pipe railing, check-plate floors, and steel columns are each painted a different color.*
Photo: Edward Jacoby

Opposite: *The interior of the lobby employs an industrial aesthetic of exposed, unadorned materials.*
Photo: Edward Jacoby

Overleaf: *The exterior expresses the non-differentiated spaces of the loft located behind the walls.*
Photo: Edward Jacoby

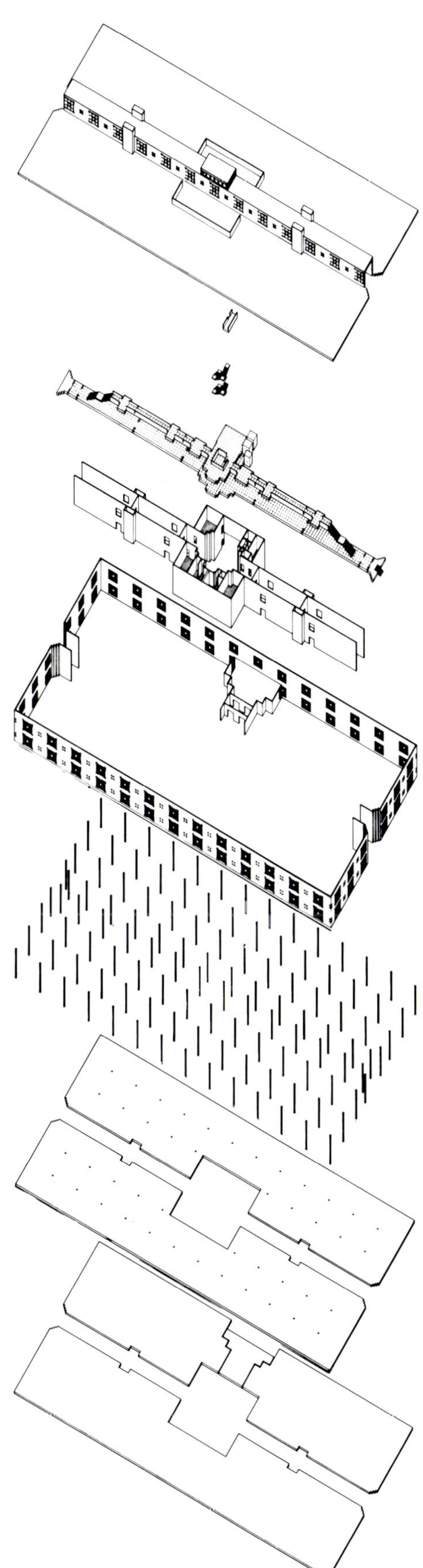

AXONOMETRIC

ENOCH PRATT
FREE LIBRARY

This 1933 public library needed interior and exterior restoration to bring it up to current building codes and to make it a vital resource for the community it serves. An initial feasibility study found the structure to be generally sound with the architectural detail, masonry, and woodwork in good shape but in need of refurbishing. The program included expanded floor space for popular collections, redesigned offices, new information areas, and a signage system.

Eleven thousand square feet of new stack space was created through the careful insertion of four mezzanines into the main reading room. One of the primary design goals was to integrate the new mezzanines with the old structure. Four new interior entrance "portals" clearly define the four major departments of the library—Fiction, Science, History, and Government Documents. The mezzanines and portals are finished in marble, Honduran mahogany, brass, and etched glass and they are detailed to match the library's existing architecture.

The library's central hall was restored and refinished, the walls selectively repainted, the marble cleaned and repaired, and the luminous ceiling restored with new glazing. A new information kiosk of marble and bronze is now a feature of the central hall.

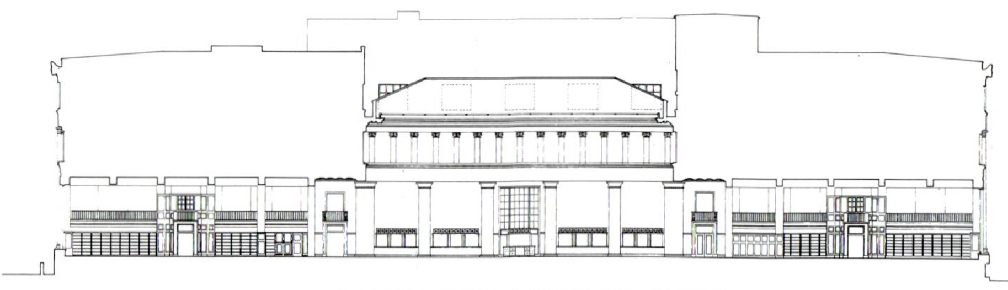

LONGITUDINAL SECTION LOOKING EAST

Above: *The library's exterior expresses the simplified Classicism popular in public buildings during the Depression.*
Photo: Richard Mandelkorn

Opposite Page: *(top) The vestibule features a new, glassed-in guard kiosk of brass and marble.*
Photo: Richard Mandelkorn
(bottom) One of four entry portals to the library's major departments, the doorway is made of etched glass, marble, brass, and mahogany.
Photo: Richard Mandelkorn
**in association with Ayers/Saint/Gross, Baltimore, MD*

Overleaf Photo: Richard Mandelkorn

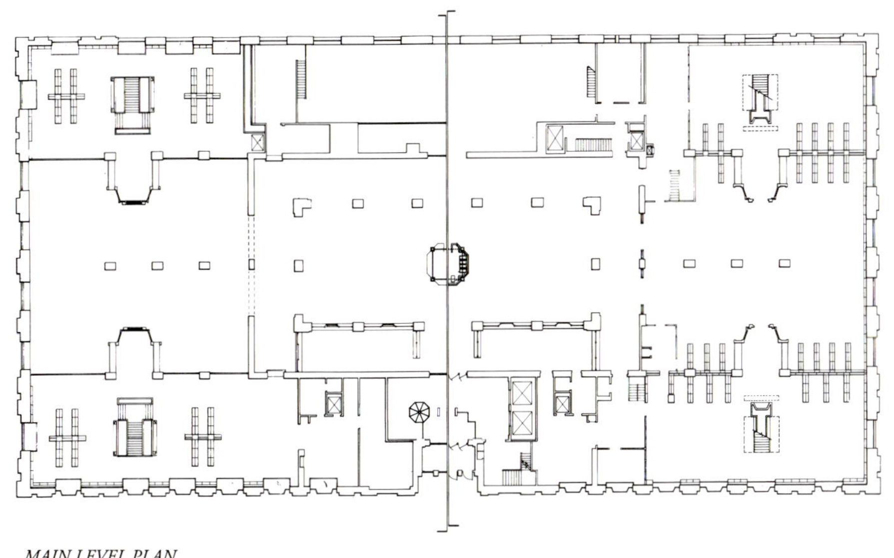

MAIN LEVEL PLAN

WILLIAM
NUTHEAD

THE
SEELEY G. MUDD
CHEMISTRY
BUILDING
1984

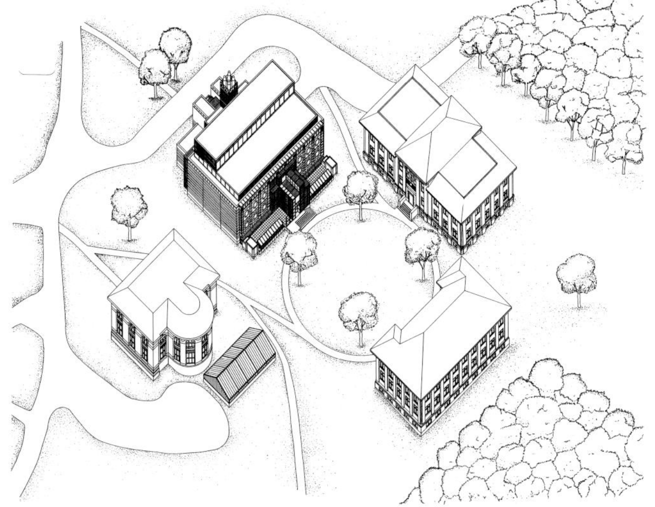

AXONOMETRIC

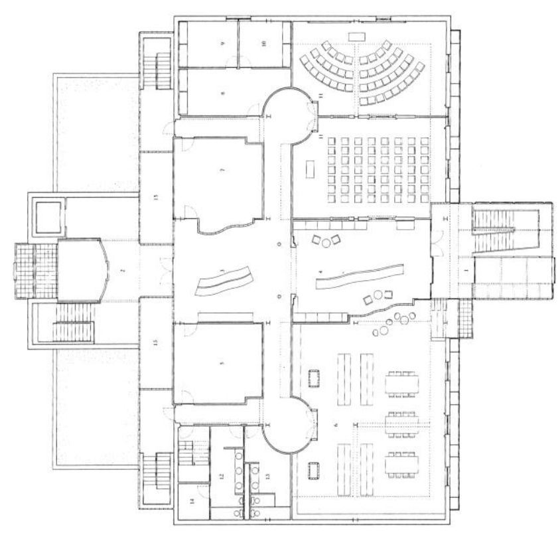

UPPER LEVEL

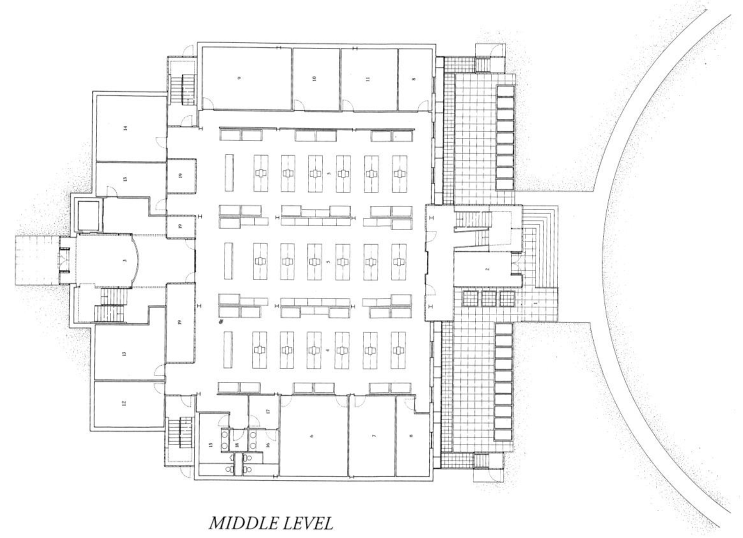

MIDDLE LEVEL

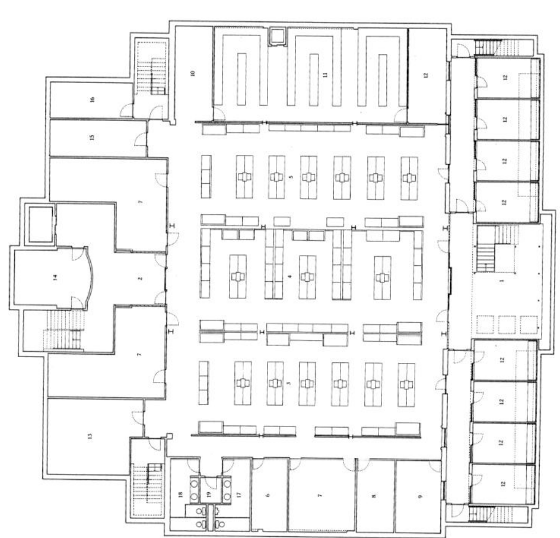

LOWER LEVEL

Left: *The axial front entrance on the north elevation reaches out to greet the visitor with a glass-block portal.*
Photo: Peter Vanderwarker

Overleaf: *The Mudd Chemistry Building at Vassar shares its palette of materials with the surrounding context.*
Photo: Peter Vanderwarker

LOWELL MEMORIAL AUDITORIUM

Originally built as a war veterans memorial in 1927, the auditorium had been neglected for over 25 years. The initial feasibility and programming study involved civic, cultural, institutional, and business groups: the architects' ability to coordinate the interests of those groups was key in the city's successful application for state funding.

The exterior of the building was cleaned, and the entrances were redesigned. Interiors were completely refurbished and reworked to meet new program needs. The stage was enlarged in order to accommodate theatrical productions, and the original seats were removed, refinished, reupholstered, and reconfigured. The seats were eliminated from a 12-foot zone around the periphery of the auditorium

and the floor was made level in order to increase the flexibility of the space. New mechanical, electrical, acoustical, and lighting systems were installed, new floors and finishes were added, and the walls and ceilings were acoustically treated. The building also houses a wing of offices and a smaller theater which is the home of the Merrimac Repertory Theater Company.

While the auditorium was redesigned to meet modern demands, the spirit and grace of the original classical architecture was not violated. Two new terraces which flank the building serve as pre-function areas and provide access for the disabled. The building has been restored to its original grandeur and has once again become a major cultural center of the city.

Above: *As part of the restoration project, the auditorium's exterior was cleaned and new flanking terraces were added for accessibility for persons with disabilities.*
Photo: Richard Mandelkorn

Right: *An overview of the newly restored auditorium from the balcony. Many of the original features, such as the pendant fixtures, were maintained.*
Photo: Richard Mandelkorn

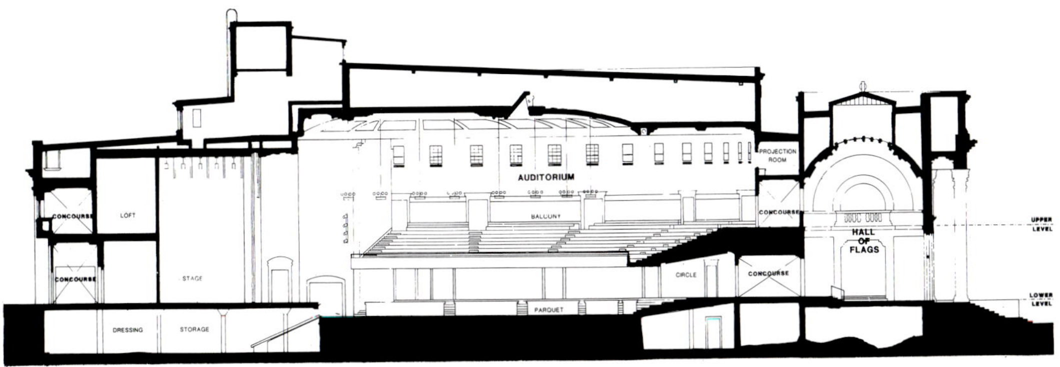

LONGITUDINAL SECTION

Above: *A view of the lobby from mezzanine level reveals the intricately detailed, plaster barrel vault.*
Photo: Richard Mandelkorn

Below: *Skylights crown the vaulted plaster ceiling in another view of the lobby.*
Photo: Richard Mandelkorn

Opposite Page: *Access to the parquet level was achieved with an unobtrusive ramp and brass railing.*
Photo: Richard Mandelkorn

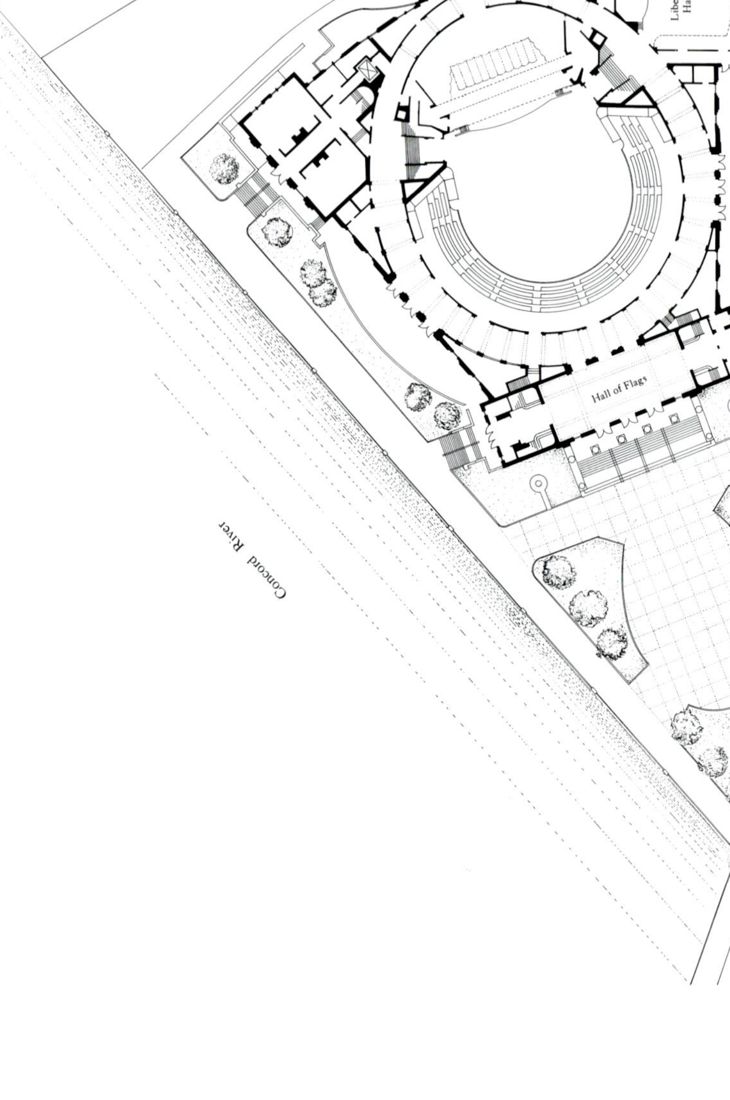

OLIN MEMORIAL LIBRARY

A major renovation and addition to this college library, originally designed by McKim, Mead & White, was the answer to Wesleyan University's overcrowded and outdated library system. Built in 1923 and standing majestically in the center of campus, the library had an architectural integrity and symbolic importance that demanded sensitive treatment. The university wanted to preserve the original style and presence of the building while updating it. The project included renovation of 65,000 square feet and the addition of 35,000 square feet of new space.

The addition gracefully wraps around the north facade of the original library, which now functions as an interior wall of a new triple-height reading room. The reading room is the primary space where new meets old, while it balances the elegant lobby on the south side. Large expanses of glass create a space which is light and inviting and which allows views across the field and campus beyond.

Mezzanines were inserted between the second and third levels and the third and attic levels to allow for future stack expansion. Study carrels line the connection between the old and new buildings and dramatically overlook the reading room. The seating capacity of the library was increased from 280 to 620.

The addition was designed with respect for the original library and the site. The new facade echoes the original which is visible behind it. The original arched windows are projected onto the new facade and classical motifs are reinterpreted in contemporary materials. The north elevation bends with a gentle curve in order to diminish the perceived mass of the building and in deference to the library's neighbors. Its design is in sympathy with the rhythms of solids and voids made by the original structures on Brownstone Row, which bound Andrus Field to the east and set the urban style of the campus. The new library forms a backdrop to Dennison Terrace, the traditional setting for Wesleyan commencements.

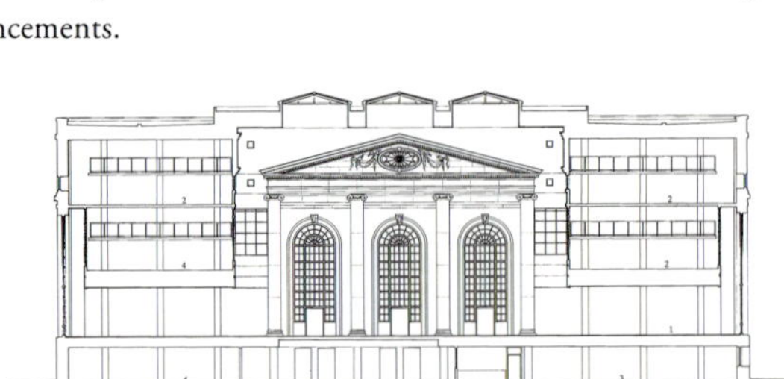

SECTION

Above: *Secluded, third-floor reading areas are pulled back from the new exterior wall containing arch-top windows.*
Photo: Steve Rosenthal

Right: *Viewed at night, the addition reveals the large reading room inside, with its brick interior wall.*
Photo: Steve Rosenthal

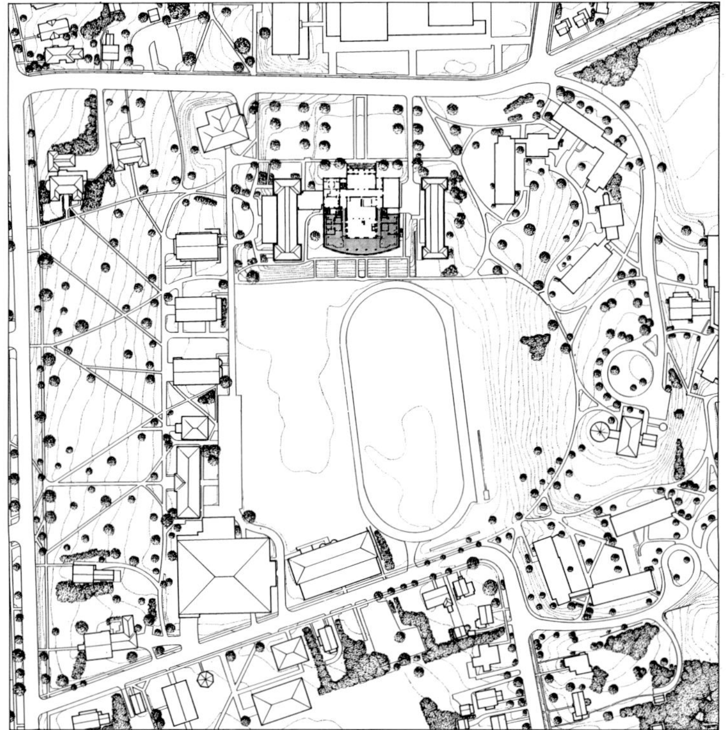

SITE PLAN

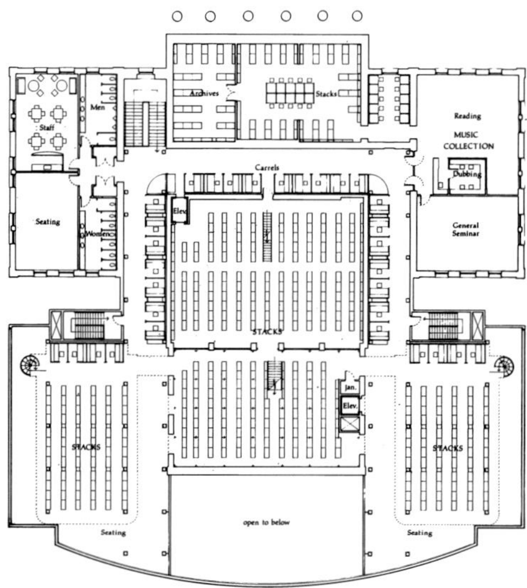

THIRD FLOOR

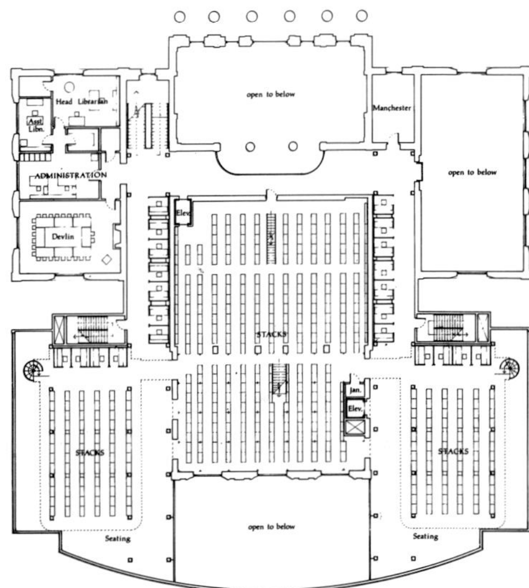

SECOND FLOOR

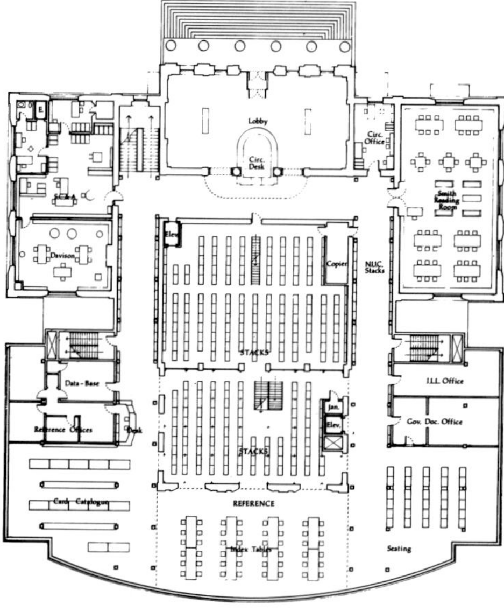

FIRST FLOOR

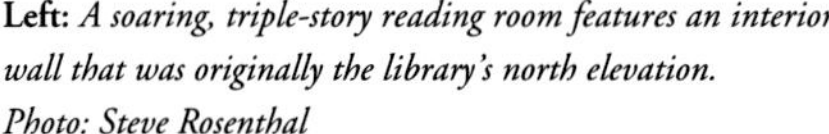

Left: *A soaring, triple-story reading room features an interior wall that was originally the library's north elevation.*
Photo: Steve Rosenthal

Overleaf: *As it faces Andrus Field to the north, the shape of the library addition follows a gentle curve.*
Photo: Steve Rosenthal

CAMPUS CENTER

When Amherst College began phasing out its student fraternities, they found a need for a new focal point for academic life—a place where students and faculty could gather and interact. The design intent was to create an architectural expression of the spirit of collegiality that should fill undergraduate life.

This 35,000-square-foot campus center is sited on a graceful sloping lawn with expansive views of the hills to the south. Its front facade stands two stories high, with a large, inviting plaza for outdoor gatherings; the building is a symmetrical interpretation of the Colonial mansions found in the village of Amherst. From the southeast, the rear of the building with its balconies, trellised porches, and loggia beckons students from the residence halls as they start

out in the morning. Students and faculty converge upon this oversized "country home" throughout the day to socialize and meet in its campus store, post office, coffee shops, game rooms, music rooms, study lounges, faculty conference rooms, and student organization offices.

At the center of the biaxial plan a single volume projects the full height of the main gable, and from this room every major function area can be reached. It assumes an urban role at the heart of the building and campus—a forum for campus life. In the same way that the Amherst campus is arranged into a series of quadrangles, spaces are arranged around the forum. Spatial sequences reflect social purposes, accommodating both chance encounters and formal gatherings. The campus center acts as a living room for the college.

Architectural forms and materials are derived from the college context; sandstruck brick with red mortar, a standing seam metal roof, dark green painted-wood windows in double-square vertical proportions, granite and terra cotta trim, and a white painted wood pergola.

SECTION

Above: *The yellow stucco form, which surmounts a granite base, recalls one of the campus' historic buildings.*
Photo: Richard Mandelkorn

Opposite Page: *The main entry to the student center is approached on axis from the west, across a generous terrace.*
Photo: Richard Mandelkorn

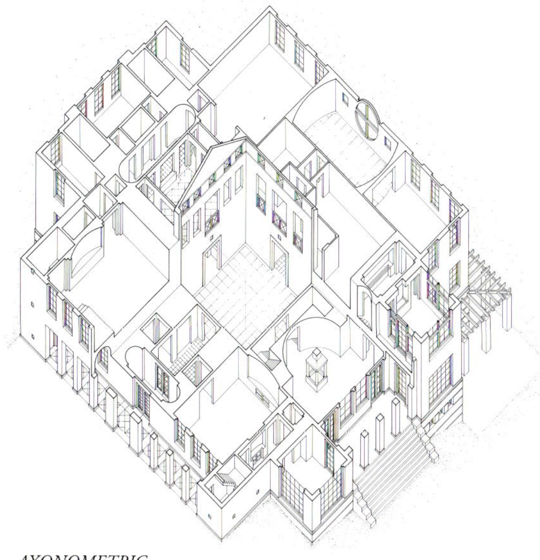

AXONOMETRIC

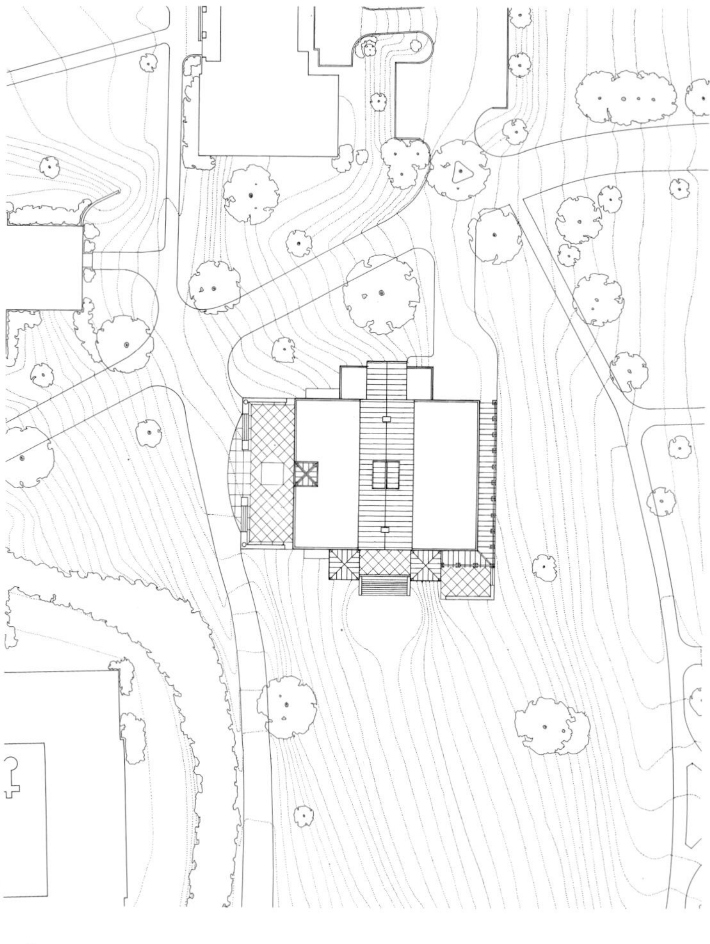

SITE PLAN

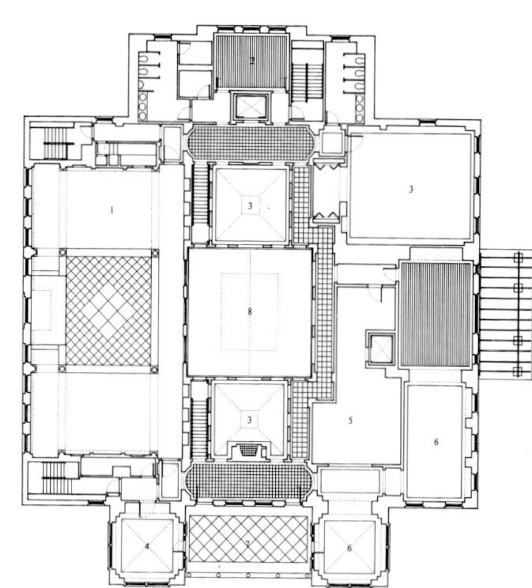

SECOND FLOOR PLAN

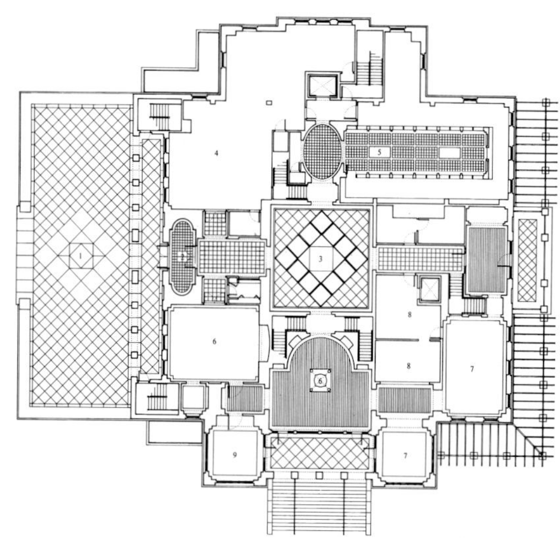

FIRST FLOOR PLAN

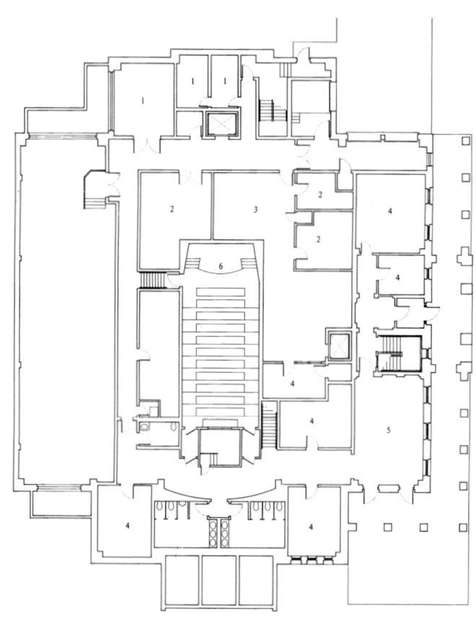

GROUND FLOOR PLAN

Left: *The three-story central space orients visitors and serves as the campus "living room."*
Photo: Richard Mandelkorn

Overleaf: *From the southeast, student dormitory side of campus, the center appears as a large mansion.*
Photo: Richard Mandelkorn

ROE VISUAL ARTS
BUILDING

The primary thrust of the design of this 29,000-square-foot visual arts center was to create a utilitarian building that would also offer a stimulating environment for the study of art. Although the materials are modest, one notices ironies and contrasts that are intended to provoke thought about issues relevant to art and architecture, such as scale, symmetry, light, and color.

Sited on a palatial campus, the building houses fully equipped ceramics, sculpture, printmaking, painting, and photography studios, a 1,200-square-foot gallery with special temperature and humidity controls, a lecture room with a remote controlled audio-visual system, five faculty offices with attached studios, a student lounge, and a 7,000-square-foot sculpture courtyard. A separate building houses a foundry and kilns.

The building is simply organized in a bi-symmetrical cross plan. The principal organizing element is a 25-foot-high east-west corridor along which the studios and classrooms are located. This colorful, light-filled corridor also serves as exhibit space for student work. The corridor skylight is glazed on the north face of the ridge, with intermittent glazing on the south face in order to produce a contrast between a continuous wash of light and shafts of light. The height and width of the corridor are modulated to produce a spatial sequence, culminating in a rotunda at the crossing of the axes.

Faculty studios, administrative offices, a seminar room, and a faculty lounge are clustered at the cross-axis. All of the studios face north and have large expanses of glazing on the north side. A mezzanine runs along the corridor wall of each of the studios taking advantage of the height of the space and serving as studio space for advanced students.

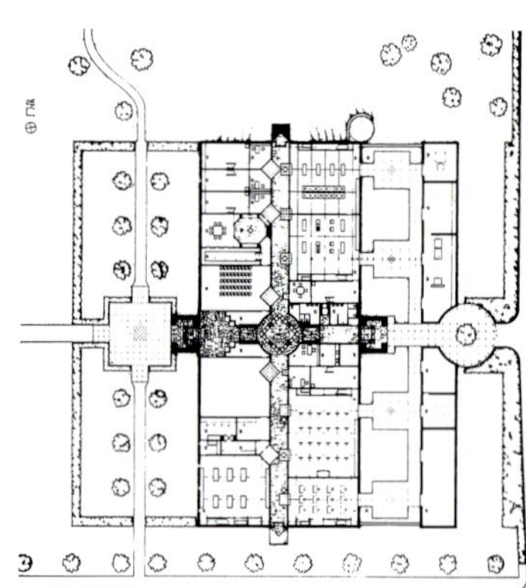

Above: *The building presents a virtually blank brick facade as it faces the Furman campus.*
Photo: Peter Vanderwarker

Right: *The entry is marked by a gabled roof and an elaborate plaque announcing the building's name.*
Photo: Peter Vanderwarker

THOMAS
ANDERSON
ROE

ART
BUILDING

AXONOMETRIC

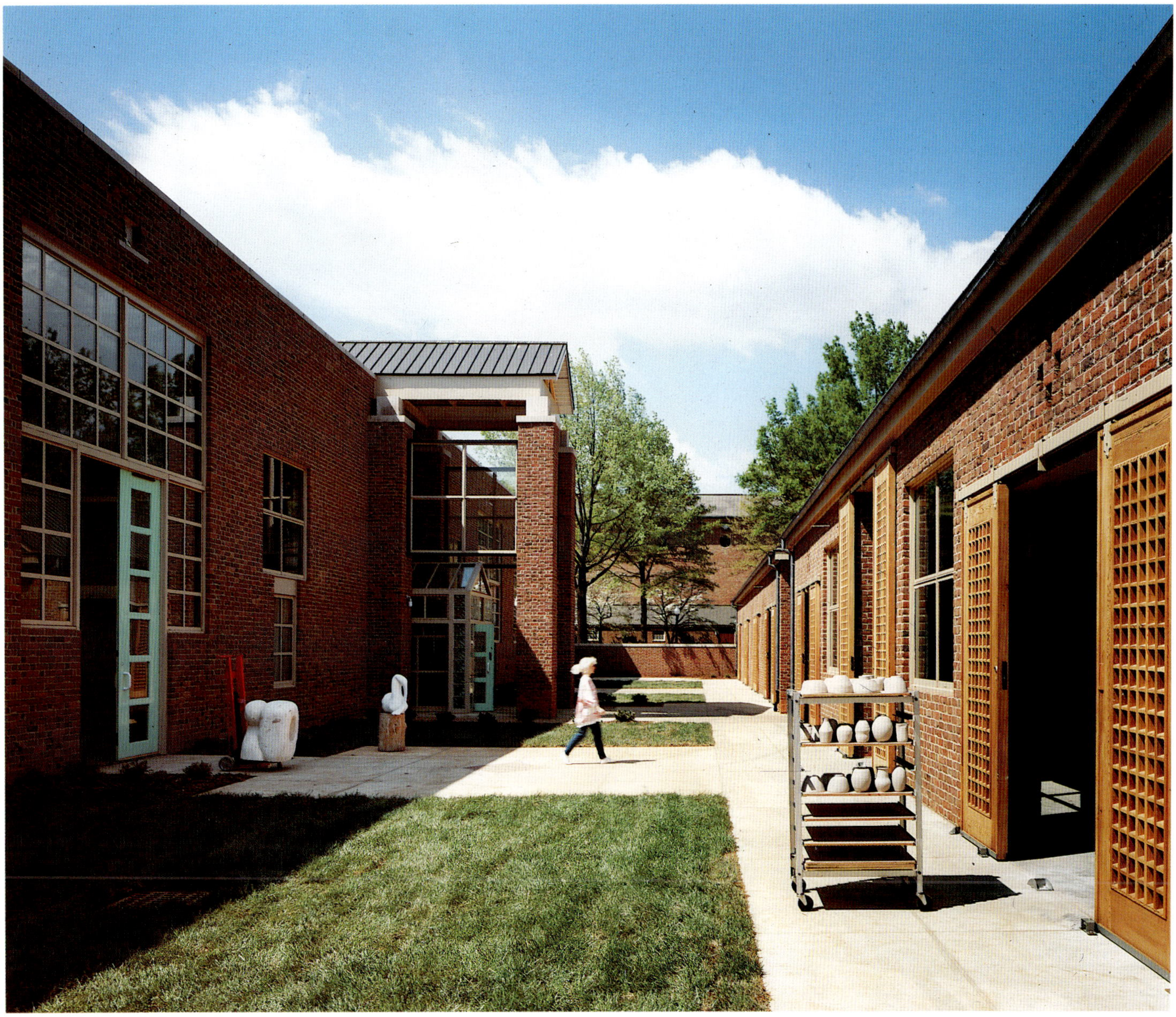

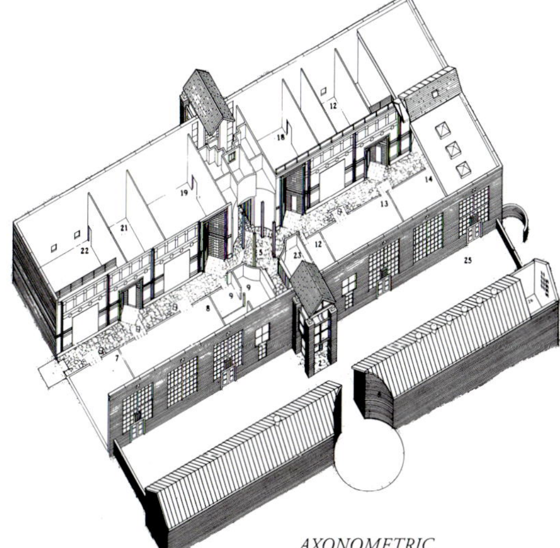

Above: *The pottery kilns and foundry are located on the building's north side, in a separate structure accessible from the studios. Photo: Peter Vanderwarker*

Left: *The central spine is a tall, light-filled space, punctuated by blue lights at the top of the walls. Photo: Peter Vanderwarker*

CORPORATE HEADQUARTERS AND EMPLOYEE RESTAURANT

This corporate and operations center includes employee services designed to meet the needs of busy personnel at the Stop & Shop corporate headquarters and the Bradlees Company offices and distribution center. Because the center is located away from the city business district, the 140-seat dining facility combines elements of a traditional employee dining space with additional on-site amenities such as a convenience store, a bank teller-machine, and private dining/conference rooms in order to offer more resources often found in an urban environment.

Designed with a traditional influence, the facility features custom, natural oak millwork; a rich yet subtle color palette of furnishings and fabrics; the abun-

dant use of plants; and a corporate art program, all designed to create the ambiance of a fine restaurant. The realities of high traffic patterns are addressed practically, with appropriate use of quarry tile and attractive carpeting. Equally effective is the varied employment of recessed lighting and architectural details, such as custom lighting valences and columns.

The theme of the design is a rich palette of elements employed in contrasting ways. Dark colors are used in unison with light woodwork, direct lighting is balanced with indirect illumination. Light color floor coverings are juxtaposed to dark colors, and solid partitions are balanced with interior windows permitting views throughout the headquarters. These contrasting devices enliven the interior and help to differentiate spaces.

The open area of the dining room is subdivided by a hierarchy of architectural details; low planters, varied ceiling heights, and oak columns of differing heights define intimate eating areas. Large windows, cut into the original wall, allow views out to adjacent conservation lands.

Above: *In the dining room, low planters, varied ceiling and column heights achieve more intimate eating areas.*
Photo: Richard Mandelkorn

Right: *Interior windows are used to permit views between spaces and to share light.*
Photo: Richard Mandelkorn

DAVENPORT STUDENT CENTER

This conversion of a vacant 1903 classroom building into a new student center at Wesleyan University has filled this nearly century-old structure with new life and has provided the academic community with a new meeting center.

The building houses a variety of spaces—cafeteria, coffee house, pub, "cabaret," student store, post office, and meeting rooms—and encourages social interaction of all types, from very casual and spontaneous to more formal and organized. The spaces have been organized so that the most heavily used spaces are located on the lower floors. As one moves up through the building the spaces become quieter and more private, terminating in a rooftop coffee house.

Many original details were preserved or reused in surprising and delightful

ways. For example, the original staircase serves as an ordering device for the building with each new space carefully related to the stair. The counterpoint of new and old elements is whimsical and has infused the space with a luxurious, contemporary spirit. Original materials, such as exposed brick, oak, and slate play off modern ones, such as glass block, exposed steel, and neon tubing. Large voids in the walls and floors open up the spaces and give the campus center the feeling of a theatrical stage set. A muted pastel color palette evokes the early 20th Century and contributes to the building's richness.

The success of the new campus center is clear from the new pathways which have been worn across lawns to the building from all directions.

Above: *The student center's original exterior was retained, while new, light-filled spaces were created within.*
Photo: Peter Vanderwarker

Opposite Page: *(top) The cabaret is a double-height space with a mezzanine of exposed steel and glass block.*
Photo: Peter Vanderwarker
(bottom) The ground-floor lounge is a double-height space with a floating mezzanine.
Photo: Peter Vanderwarker

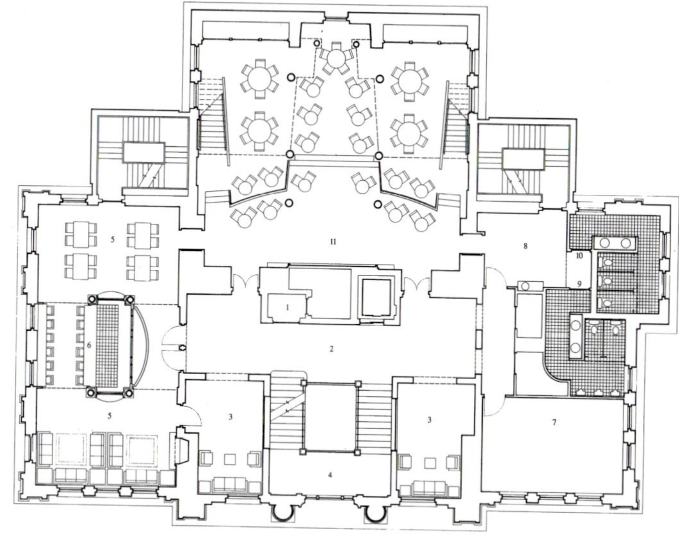

1. Tickets
2. Main Hall
3. Loggia
4. Stair Hall
5. Lounge
6. Pub
7. Game Room
8. Vestibule
9. Men
10. Women
11. Cabaret

SECOND FLOOR PLAN

PRIVATE CLUB

The interiors of this distinguished Boston private social club have been redesigned by Perry Dean Rogers & Partners over several years. Located in Back Bay within a historic building by McKim, Mead & White, the club's refurbishment has included meeting rooms, dining rooms, function rooms, offices, hallways, rest rooms, and miscellaneous spaces.

Most of these interior projects have had budget constraints but have involved every facet of design, including installation of room finishes, custom and temporary carpet, window treatments, new furniture, refurbished and reupholstered furniture, lighting, custom millwork, restoration of original finishes, paneling, lighting of artwork, tabletop design, and china selection. The approach throughout the design highlights the existing architectural details of ample crown moldings, wainscotting, and baseboards. A palette of dark colors, bright metalwork, highlighting, and rich fabrics works in unison with the interior architecture.

Variations on a single theme of colors is used throughout, allowing furniture to be used in various locations. In the Main Dining Room, updated lighting, carpeting, furnishings, window treatments, and accessories were integrated with the existing antiques, furniture, artwork, and architectural details. Construction in the Main Dining Room was coordinated so that all product and custom-fabricated items were complete and on-site before the space was closed off and demolition begun. The room has retained its traditional Edwardian design and character while receiving a timely rejuvenation.

Above: *The main dining room is framed within three separate spaces.*
Photo: Richard Mandelkorn

Right: *Smaller spaces within the main dining room offer an intimate setting for gatherings.*
Photo: Richard Mandelkorn

FIRESTONE RESIDENCE

A couple who are champion horse breeders wanted to develop 2,000 acres of rolling pasture land in Virginia for an estate that would be comfortable, elegant, non-ostentatious, and sympathetic to the natural landscape.

The site is characterized by pastures bordered with dark-stained oak fences, and interspersed with groves of hardwoods. Views feature racetracks, barns, a Black Angus farm, and the ambling Catoctin River.

The 34,000-square-foot main house is designed using elements of the traditional farmhouses in the area—stone, exposed rough-hewn beams, and pitched roofs. Thereby the large structure has residential scale and, by association with vernacular architecture, is visually at ease with the landscape.

One approaches the house via a winding road that offers glimpses of the gabled south facade as it surmounts a knoll. The drive leads to a motor court on the north side, which is framed by a garage to the east and an indoor pool structure to the west. From the entry, the house reaches out into the landscape. Long corridors off a trophy gallery at the foyer stretch east to an arcade and outdoor pavilion, while entertaining spaces open up on the sunny south side.

Colors throughout the house are reminiscent of hunt clubs, with dark hues contrasting with light woodwork. Rough stonework is also used inside, recalling the material that is the predominant feature of the exterior.

Above: *Dark colors and woodwork in the kitchen give the interior the atmosphere of a hunt club.*
Photo: Richard Mandelkorn

Right: *From the northwest, the siting of the indoor poolhouse anchors the estate in the landscape.*
Photo: Richard Mandelkorn

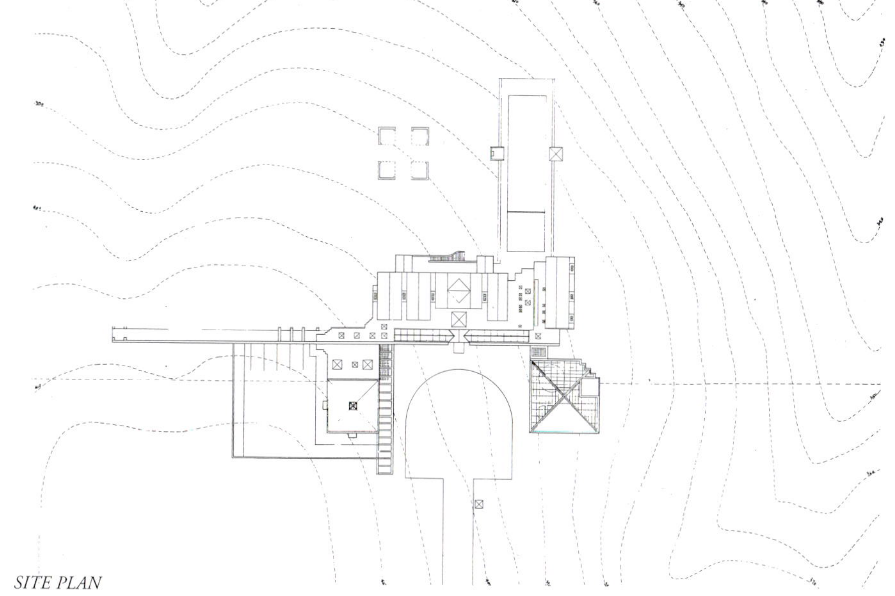

SITE PLAN

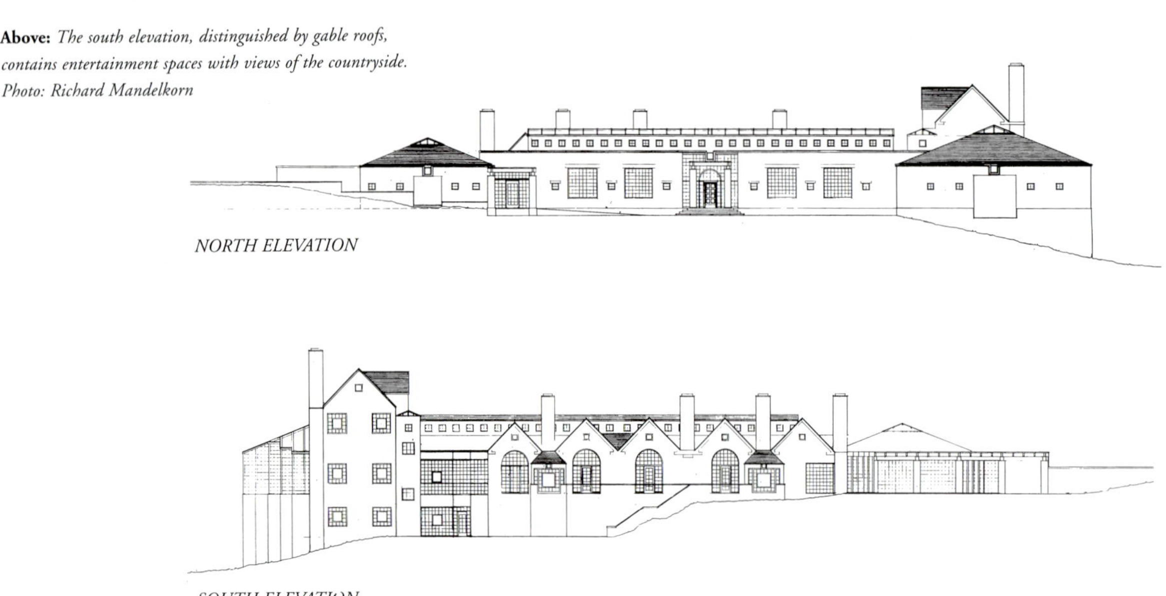

Above: *The south elevation, distinguished by gable roofs,*
contains entertainment spaces with views of the countryside.
Photo: Richard Mandelkorn

NORTH ELEVATION

SOUTH ELEVATION

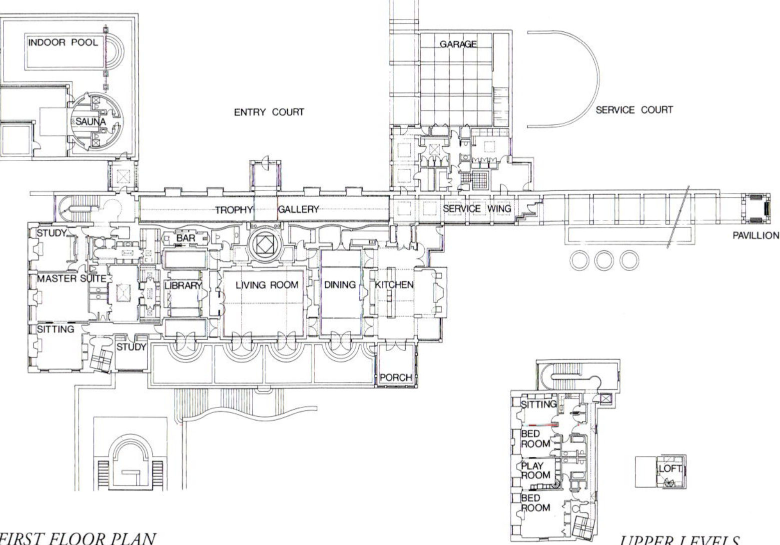

Above: *The service wing and the pergola stretch to the east.*
The windowed volume at left is a sunny breakfast nook.
Photo: Richard Mandelkorn

Overleaf: *The Firestone estate as viewed from the southwest,*
with the indoor poolhouse to the left and the bathing pavilion
to the right.
Photo: Richard Mandelkorn

FIRST FLOOR PLAN   *UPPER LEVELS*

HAMILTON COLLEGE POOL

Hamilton College, a small, private college in upstate New York, was founded in 1812 through an endowment from Alexander Hamilton. Its campus is noted for many fine, old buildings built of locally quarried stone. The college's existing 25-yard pool and pool house, built circa 1938, had slowly deteriorated. This drafty, leaky facility was then replaced with a new, larger NCAA-regulation competition pool and recreation facility.

Visitors enter the pool facility along a corridor whose gently curving exterior wall shimmers with glass block. The polygonal lobby displays swimming and diving trophies. The pool's seating area, opposite large areas of clear glass, permits views out over the green expanses of the football field.

The exposed steel structural elements of the poolhouse are finished in white and support a natural cedar deck that is part of the roof assembly. The exposed steel also emphasizes the height and openness of the natatorium. Walls in a rich yellow color make a warm background for the white, blue, red, black, and aqua tile.

The artificial lighting is both high intensity sodium over the decks (to keep skin tones looking natural) and high intensity mercury over the water to provide the mandatory 100 foot-candles at the surface.

Above: *The fenestration creates a lively wall of color and light at the north end of the poolhouse.*
Photo: Richard Mandelkorn

Right: *A combination of clear and opaque glass in the windows permits and obscures enticing views of the interior.*
Photo: Richard Mandelkorn

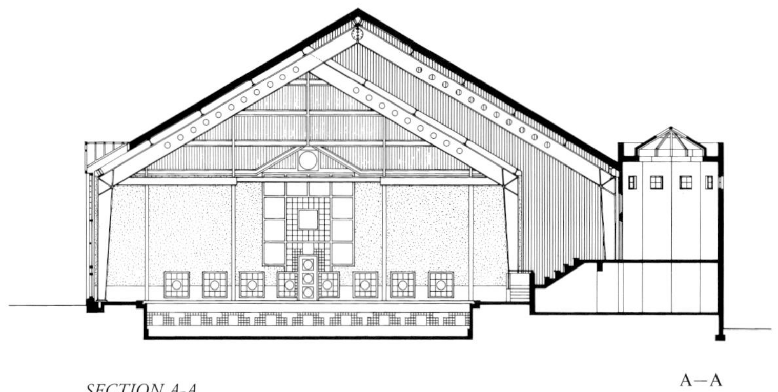

SECTION A-A

A—A

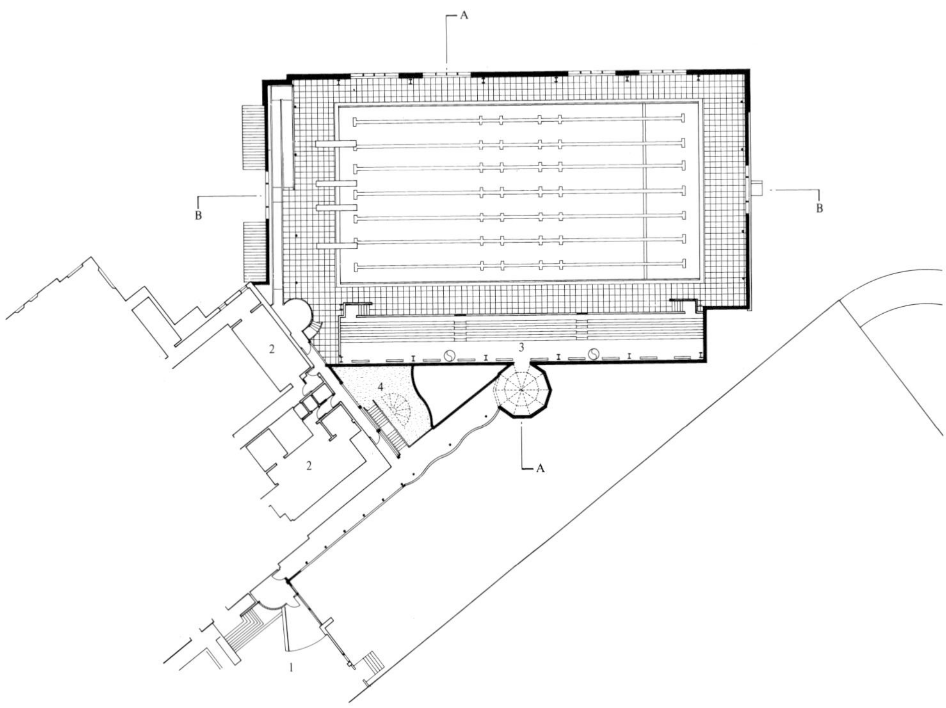

FLOOR PLAN

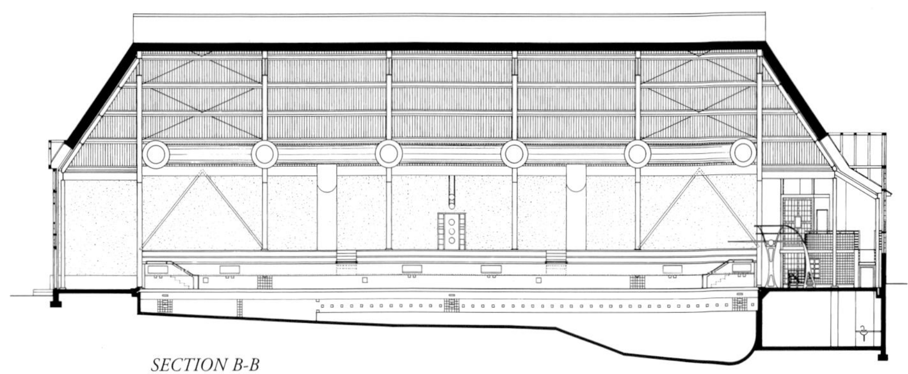

SECTION B-B

Left: *At night, the building glows, making the poolhouse a campus landmark.*
Photo: Richard Mandelkorn

Above: *A ramp at the south end of the poolhouse delivers visitors from the existing building to the new enclosure.*
Photo: Richard Mandelkorn

Right: *Cladding of simple materials is used on the exterior to contrast with the highly articulated windows.*
Photo: Richard Mandelkorn

Below: *The entry corridor leads to a polygonal antechamber just outside the pool seating area.*
Photo: Richard Mandelkorn

Opposite Page: *A view of the poolhouse's east wall demonstrates the clear articulation of the steel structure and the interior wood ceiling.*
Photo: Richard Mandelkorn

ELIZABETH PARKS
KILLIAN HALL

This renovation of the former Hayden Gallery at the Massachusetts Institute of Technology has transformed an exhibition space into a 3,500-square-foot hall designed for musical events and for small formal gatherings. Elizabeth Parks Killian Hall, as it is now known, is technically fitted to provide excellent acoustic conditions for a variety of performance settings.

The installation of 10 large, hinged panels of hard finish mahogany permits the acoustic tuning of this elegant space. The panels can be adjusted like shutters to different angles to achieve just the right acoustical effect for a variety of performances. The room does not, however, reflect a sacrifice of aesthetics to address acoustical requirements. A rich palette of mauve and cream creates an intimate environment; textured carpeting and mahogany paneling distinguish the space. Fabric-covered chrome stacking chairs and a demountable wood floor permit a variety of performance formats.

Although it is designed primarily for the performance of chamber music ensembles, the hall will also accommodate receptions, lectures, film screenings, and the archival recording of student performances. The installation of recording facilities in an upstairs control room and a screen room on the bottom floor to accommodate performers makes this three-story facility a state-of-the-art addition to MIT.

Above: *Fabric-covered chrome stacking chairs and a demountable wood floor permit a variety of performance formats.*
Photo: Richard Mandelkorn

Right: *Hinged panels of mahogany and fabric allow the space to be "tuned" for the specific needs of performances.*
Photo: Richard Mandelkorn

HENDERSON CANDLER ASSOCIATES SHOWROOM

The client for this 2,700-square-foot showroom lacked a specific unified market identity and as a result required a cost effective, high impact design solution for their showroom. The modest budget of $11 per square foot necessitated the use of inexpensive materials in unexpected and innovative ways.

A dramatic entrance draws visitors into the showroom, which is situated at the end of a long corridor at the Boston Design Center. A forced perspective is created by two converging rows of clear, corrugated fiberglass panels used as backdrops for seating displays. The panels are framed with standard aluminum ridge-roll flashing, mounted vertically on copper tube poles. The double row of fiberglass and chairs leads the visitor back to a niche created by a curved rear wall, which provides a backdrop for special display pieces.

A central display island was created, using ebony and natural patio block, the edge of which is ragged on one side to help draw visitors back to the conference area. On vertical surfaces, a large four-foot-square grid helps establish the size and scale of the furnishings, while taking full advantage of the 13-foot-high ceilings. The two private offices have partitions composed of glass and pointed millwork designed on a four-foot grid. The side display window features a large 12-foot-square violet wall with copper mounts and aluminum pipe detailing the grid lines. Small and large copper rings hang from the pipe, like ornaments on a large necklace. These copper rings allow the owners to cascade fabrics for display.

The showroom's color palette enhances both wooden case goods and upholstered products. The color scheme incorporates bold accents of violet, ochre, and terra cotta. Dramatic sparkle is obtained through the use of copper and aluminum. Together, the balance of neutrals and saturated colors support ongoing changes in furniture and products.

Above: *The theme of the grid, which organizes the interior design, is established at the entry to the showroom.*
Photo: Richard Mandelkorn

Right: *A forced perspective is created by two converging rows of clear corrugated fiberglass panels used as backdrops for seating displays.*
Photo: Richard Mandelkorn

GENERAL MAIL FACILITY

The USPS General Mail Facility is a 250,000-square-foot, single-level, industrial building used for the sorting, processing, and redistribution of the mail. The client wanted an economical and efficient building that would provide maximum flexibility for the mail sorting equipment over time and for future expansion. The challenge was to create architecture from a rigidly functional program for a building of large and unusual proportions.

The scale of the building on the site is vast. The main entrance facade is 400 feet long and 23 feet high and oriented perpendicular to the axis of the entrance road. The bright blue color of the elevation assumes a sculptural image across the landscape. The image is punctuated solely by a faceted glass block volume,

behind which is the lunchroom. Glass block was selected because it provides natural light with security and has a glistening presence after dark. The principal occupancy of this building occurs at night, and the glass block form functions as a beacon for incoming employees and visitors.

The plan organization reflects the functional demands of the mail processing activities. The interior is essentially one large workroom; the dimensions of the sorting area are 500 feet by 350 feet. Within this area all mail sorting activity occurs using sophisticated sorting and packaging equipment. Additional space is dedicated to employee support and supervisory areas.

The design of the building structure and systems functions as a network of overlapping grids, and is reflected in the expression of the exterior skin of the building; a preformed, ribbed-profile, steel-insulated panel system. The panels, low-cost and utilitarian, are organized into proportional squares set apart by channel reveals and accented by carefully developed rhythms of windows, loading doors, canopies, and louvers.

This building is a celebration of straightforward materials, and an honest representation of assembly and purpose.

Above: *The curving wall at the entrance incorporates glass block, clear glass, and blue glazed block.*
Photo: Steve Rosenthal

Right: *The main entrance features two entryways: one for employees and the other for management.*
Photo: Steve Rosenthal

1. General Mail Facility
2. Official Parking—35 spaces
3. Employee Parking—500 spaces
4. Truck Maneuvering Area
5. Building Expansion
6. Retention Pond
7. Existing Buildings
8. State Highway
9. Power Lines

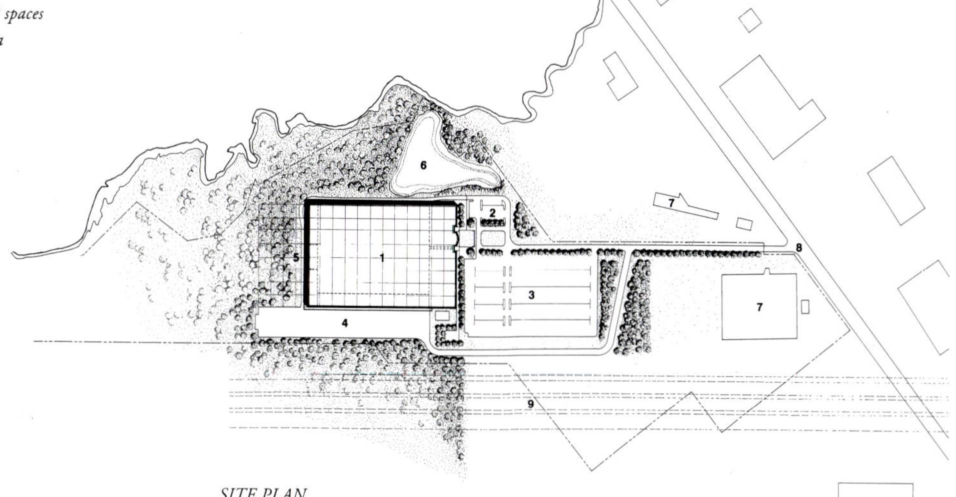

SITE PLAN

UNITED STATES POSTAL SERVICE
MIDDLESEX / ESSEX G M F

SUPERIOR COURTHOUSE

Originally constructed in 1858, the Superior Courthouse was designed by architect George Baker. The building was destroyed by a fire in 1859 and completely reconstructed the same year. The courthouse was subsequently expanded in 1902. This classical Romanesque Revival style building is noted for its decorative window detailing, stonework, a unique glass-domed atrium, and its elegant courtrooms. The structure is listed on the National Register of Historic Places.

A second fire in 1981 badly damaged the East Wing, and that portion of the building remained vacant and continued to deteriorate until the start of reconstruction. The interior of the courthouse suffered from significant fire damage. Only the skylit atrium and two courtrooms remained intact enough for renovations. The rest of the interior required extensive demolition and rebuilding.

In the process of redesign, particular attention was paid to the duplication of original details as well as to the creation of necessary spaces for a modern courthouse. The introduction of a new, intermediate floor in what was once a double height space allowed the addition of another much-needed courtroom, as well as the expansion of other ancillary spaces.

In the preservation of the exterior, many historical records were consulted in order to achieve the original roofline and shape of the 1859 structure. Some details, such as the wooden window frames, were maintained; others, such as the cornice, were replaced by modern materials molded to duplicate the original. The bricks of the new access ramp for the disabled were carefully matched to the color and type of those on the existing building, to blend the new structure with the old.

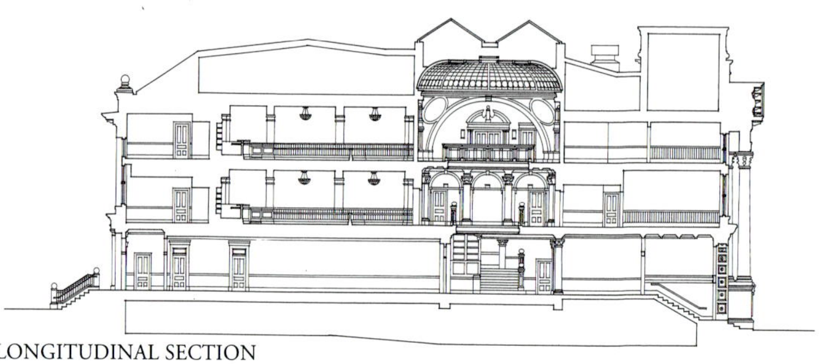

LONGITUDINAL SECTION

Above: *The glass-domed atrium was restored with attention to the original details of plaster ornament.*
Photo: Richard Mandelkorn

Right: *Ornamental metalwork in the atrium stair was part of the the courthouse's original design.*
Photo: Richard Mandelkorn

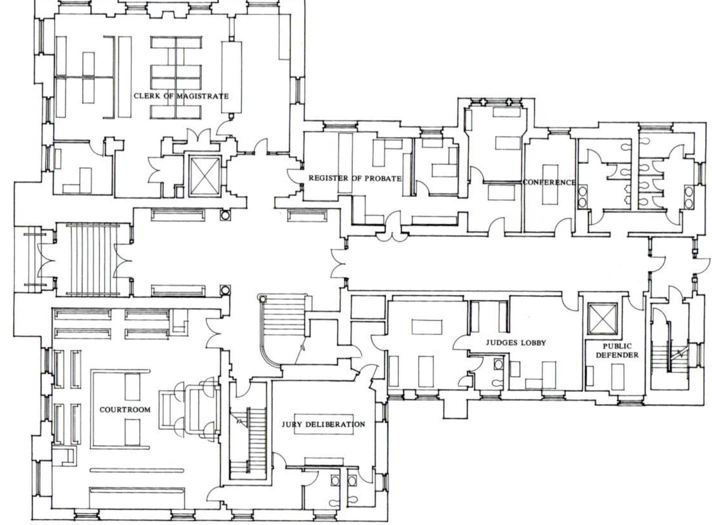

Above: *The courthouse's original drawings from the 1850s were used to make the restoration of the roofline and exterior details more authentic.*
Photo: Richard Mandelkorn

FIRST FLOOR PLAN

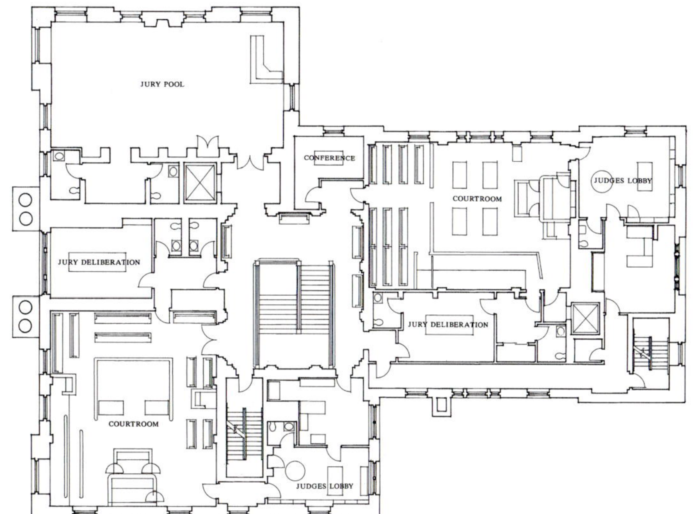

Above: *A new, third-floor courtroom was created by infilling a double-height space with an intermediate floor.*
Photo: Richard Mandelkorn

Overleaf: *The restored atrium, viewed from the mezzanine level.*
Photo: Richard Mandelkorn

SECOND FLOOR PLAN

ADDISON-WESLEY
EXECUTIVE OFFICES

The 5,000-square-foot renovation of the executive floor of Addison-Wesley Publishing Company's corporate headquarters included an elevator lobby, a cafeteria, and executive offices. The addition of a large interior window creates a visual axis from the elevator lobby through the dining room to the landscape beyond. This window also allows natural light into a formerly dark, enclosed space. The design of the elevator lobby entices the visitors with views through the space. This vista gives the impression that the office is more spacious than it actually is. Color is used judiciously, giving prominence to natural materials. Subdued shades of gray contrast with warm wood tones throughout. A large

existing cafeteria was divided into new executive offices and a smaller and more elegant dining room. The detailing and proportions of the fabric-wrapped panels, window lights, and custom-built wood planters and condiments counter are derived from the existing building's architectural vocabulary.

Above: A detail of the planter room-divider in the cafeteria features delicate wood profiles and carved rosette derived from the building's architectural ornament.
Photo: Richard Mandelkorn

Opposite Page: A new interior window permits views out to the horizon and also lets natural light penetrate deep into the space.
Photo: Richard Mandelkorn

BROODMARE
BARN

As part of a large estate, this broodmare barn is located not far from the main house. The primary purpose for the 12-sided circular training barn is to provide a safe place to exercise the new barn foals for the first few days of their lives, while they are gaining control of their balance. It also provides a place for the mares to be protected during inclement weather.

The stable takes the form of a 16-stall linear building that virtually mirrors an existing building to the south. Although functionally straightforward, the nature of the "users" presents some unique requirements for the stable. Ventilation is extremely important, as horses can produce as much as two gallons of perspiration a day. Large doors open at either end for east-west ventilation.

Windows are placed above the mare's eye level in order that she not injure herself in an attempt to get loose. The stalls are designed to be "chew proof" because horses have a tendency to gnaw on anything they can get their teeth into.

Batten patterning is featured on the windows and doors, as it is common on vernacular buildings in this part of Virginia. The training barn's fieldstone base makes reference to a silo and other, older out-buildings on the estate. The barn is crowned with a whimsical weathervane that depicts a stork carrying a diapered foal.

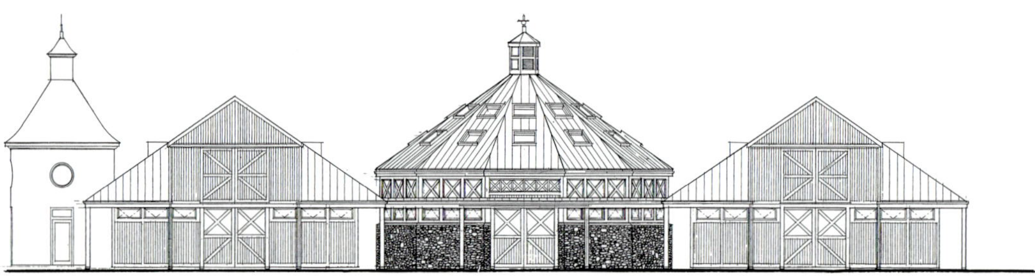

EAST ELEVATION

Above: *The symmetrical arrangement of stables and the training barn has a Palladian bearing.*
Photo: Richard Mandelkorn

Right: *Geometric patterns distinguish the ceiling of the training barn's 12-segment timber roof.*
Photo: Richard Mandelkorn

Overleaf: *The broodmare barn has a native-stone base that recalls the region's traditional architecture.*
Photo: Richard Mandelkorn

ETTINGER HALL
RENOVATION

One of the three buildings which made up the original Muhlenberg College campus, Ettinger Hall was built in 1903. The 50,000-square-foot structure, listed on the National Register of Historic Places, is Collegiate Gothic in style, and constructed of rough-cut stone with a bluestone base and limestone trim. During its long history, Ettinger has housed everything from the college chapel to the gymnasium, as well as classrooms and dormitory rooms. Now the ground floor has been renovated into a computer center, which includes the college's mainframe computer along with the computer science department and an academic computing center for student use.

A major challenge of the Ettinger renovation was making the building accessible to the disabled. Formerly, the building's main floors had been seven feet above and seven feet below grade. These floors were removed and a grade-level entry was built half-way between the ground floor and first floor.

A variety of traditional and computer-equipped classrooms occupy the first and second floors, including two tiered computer classroom laboratories. Faculty offices and suites on the first and third floors are configured to invite both departmental and interdepartmental interaction.

Above: *The north entry, adjusted to meet grade for accessibility for persons with disabilities, delivers visitors to the lobby.*
Photo: Shimer, Hedrich-Blessing

Right: *The lobby and other public spaces on the third floor are illuminated with natural light from skylights.*
Photo: Shimer, Hedrich-Blessing

EAST-WEST SECTION

HENRY M. SEYMOUR LIBRARY

Dedicated in the 1920s, the Seymour Library's original building boasts a handsome cream-colored limestone facade with castellations, perpendicular leaded-glass windows, and stately oak doors. The interior is distinguished by oak paneling and large fireplaces. Adjoining this Collegiate Gothic gem is a less sensitive, but larger wing added in the 1950s. The challenge was to organize, update, and extend the 38,000-square-foot library's capacities and systems through a careful sequence of renovations and minor additions that would allow the library to remain open during construction.

The solution focuses on the restoration of the original building, especially the central light well, and the renovation of the 1950s addition through select

interior interventions such as the special collections area and the new book/periodical colonnade on the main floor. The colonnade is part of a new axial sequence from the restored entry lobby which then proceeds through the building to a new octagonal, double-height reading room.

Executed in a palette of modern materials such as glass block as well as the traditional wood and limestone of the existing library, the addition echoes the form, texture, and scale of the old building, while maintaining its integrity as a contemporary structure. These interventions infuse a new functional order and aesthetic dignity to the spaces and serve to forge a stronger link between the two structures.

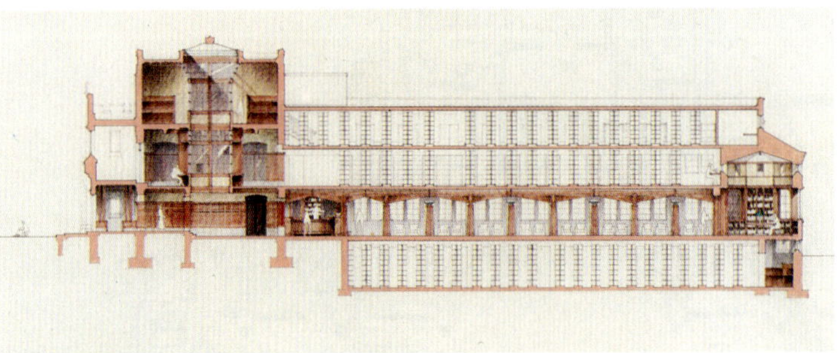

LONGITUDINAL SECTION

Above: *The elevation on the obverse side of the library's main entry expresses the volume of the octagonal reading room within.*
Photo: Shimer, Hedrich-Blessing

Right: *A view down the new axis, from the main entry toward the reading room.*
Photo: Shimer, Hedrich-Blessing

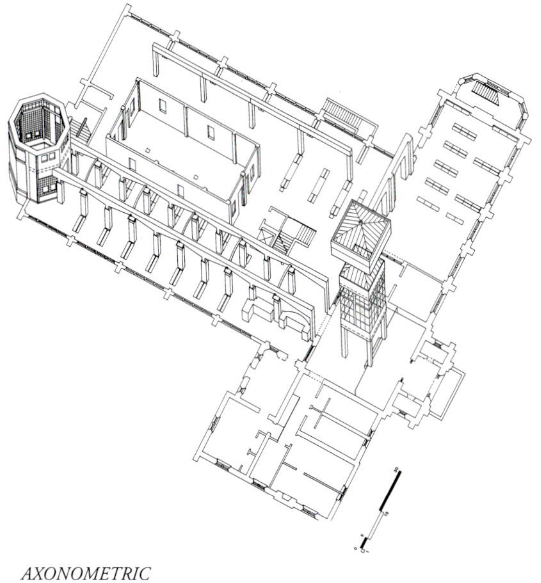

AXONOMETRIC

VILLA AMANDA

This 1,050-square-foot vacation home was designed by Frank McGuire to provide his small family with a convenient retreat from the bustle of their home on Boston's Beacon Hill. A four-acre riverside meadow located on a tidal estuary to the Atlantic Ocean was selected as the ideal site not only because of its proximity to the city, but also because of the rural flavor of the area. The former location of an 18th century boat-building concern, the site's colonial charm reminded the couple of the Tuscan countryside which had enchanted them during some years spent in Italy.

The design of this second home became an opportunity to create a Palladian-style retreat reminiscent of an Italian villa while respecting the New

England vernacular. A constraint on the site was its designation as a flood plane, therefore requiring an elevated ground floor. The initial vision of the house as "one big room" was amended during the design development phase by the arrival of a baby daughter. The original two-story format was subsequently revised to include two small bedrooms, a bath, kitchen, living area, pop-up studio, and a wrap-around roof deck.

The four-square form of Villa Amanda (named in honor of the newest addition to the family) is anchored in the Greek Revival style of the region, with biaxial symmetry and matching exterior staircases. Weathered shingle-cladding anchors the Palladian-influenced details. Pilasters of wide boards frame illusionary porticos on all sides, and cornerboards appear as rusticated quoins.

The axial plan of the house draws visitors past two small bedrooms, the kitchen and utility areas, and around the chrome-yellow chimney piece and a glossy red spiral staircase. The full length of the other side of the house is devoted to a simple living/dining room with painted-checkerboard, wooden floors. Mullioned, glazed walls take in the natural beauty of the Westport River. The upper level studio is open to the room below, with half-height walls also incorporating the Roman grills of the outside porch. This provides the vent needed to channel air through the house.

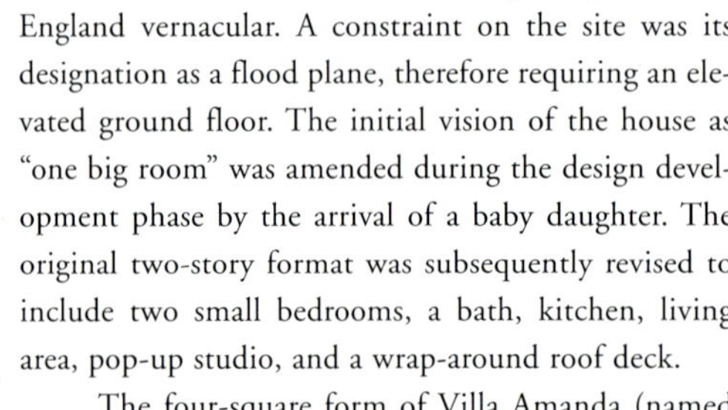

Above: *At the heart of the house, the bright yellow, double-height chimney rises into the studio space.*
Photo: Steve Rosenthal

Right: *Within the context of wild, native vegetation, the villa appears to be a pristine temple.*
Photo: Steve Rosenthal

Above: *The main living space is conceived as one large space, comprising living and dining areas, with views to the west.*
Photo: Steve Rosenthal

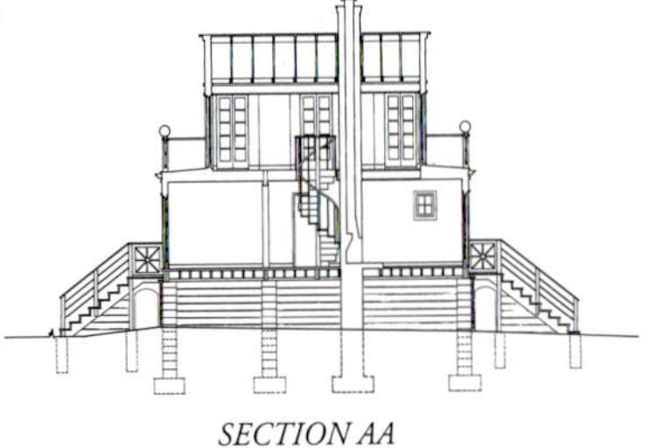

SECTION AA

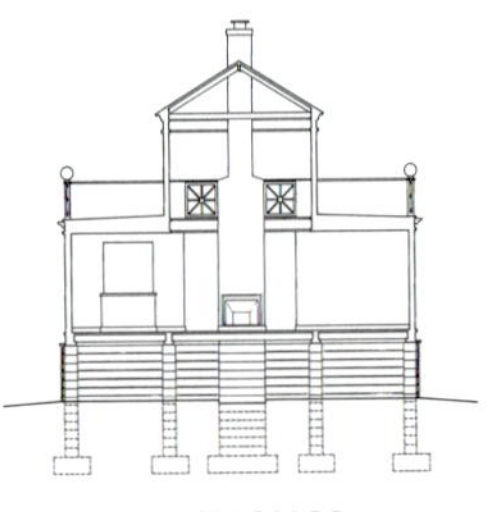

SECTION BB

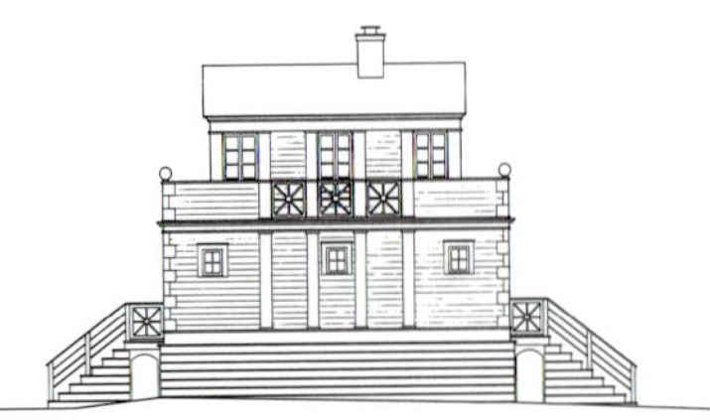

NORTH ELEVATION

WEST ELEVATION

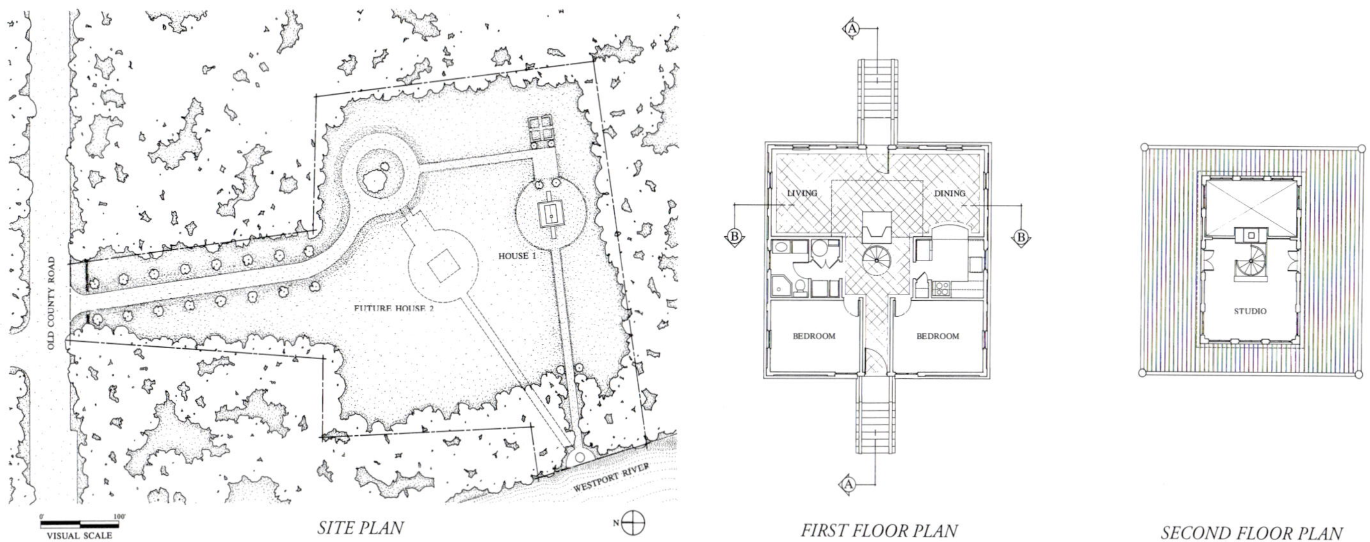

Above and Overleaf Photos: Steve Rosenthal

SITE PLAN

FIRST FLOOR PLAN

SECOND FLOOR PLAN

SAMUEL COURTNEY
RESIDENCE HALL

This residence hall occupies a three-acre site adjacent to the campus green and between two existing dormitories. The college wanted a building reminiscent of the 19th century architecture found at the school's former campus location, an architecture that contrasts markedly with the modern buildings of the newer campus. At the same time the building program required the integration of this traditional design with a completely functional 20th century interior.

This formal and symmetrical building embraces a central courtyard. Traditional design elements include a brick facade with ornamental brickwork along the first floor and at the eaves; sloped, metal roof forms recall the more costly copper roofs of an earlier era. An effort was made to reduce the scale of this 100,000-

square-foot building so as not to encroach on the lower, more modern buildings on either side. Two lower wings flank the building's tall, central entrance; together they surround the courtyard area and create the illusion of "stepping down" to the campus green. Horizontal, tricolor brick patterns on the facade further enhance the structure's seemingly low profile.

The design of the building permits more public spaces—such as student lounges and recreation rooms—to overlook the central courtyard, which is landscaped with sugar maples and English ivy. More private bedrooms and studies are located primarily at the rear of this building, to allow students to enjoy the quiet and solitude of the neighboring bluff and pine grove.

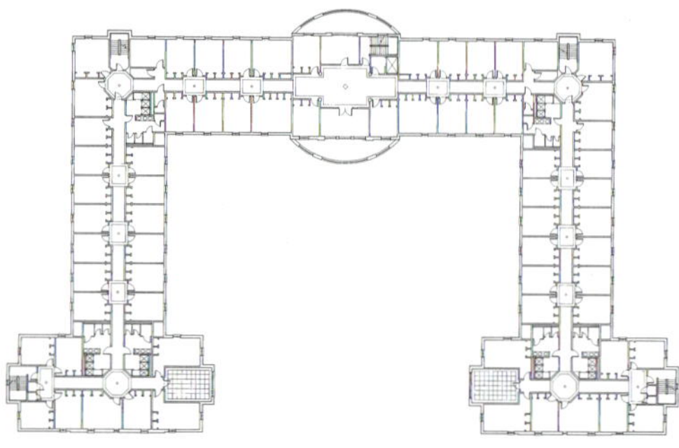

FLOOR PLAN

Above: *The formal design for the residence hall includes a facade with bricks that become lighter in color at the top.*
Photo: Richard Mandelkorn

Opposite Page: *As it faces southwest, the residence hall has the presence of a huge estate of axial symmetry.*
Photo: Richard Mandelkorn

Overleaf: *The building's solidity is reinforced by brick masses, towers, and a heavy base.*
Photo: Richard Mandelkorn

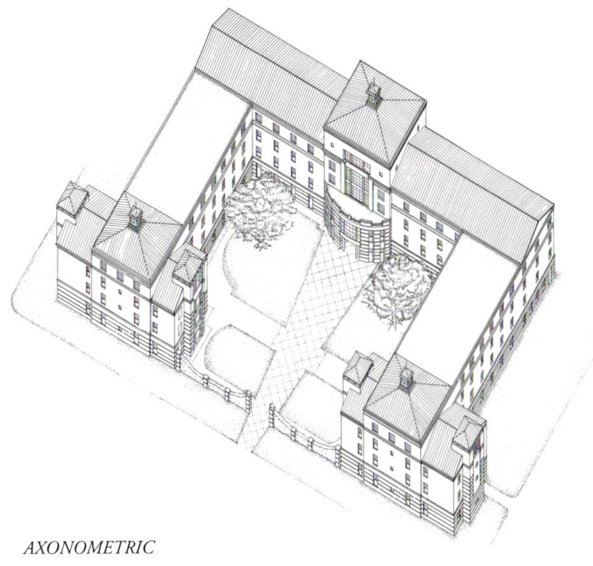

AXONOMETRIC

KREITZBERG LIBRARY

Kreitzberg Library is located near the base of a hill at the edge of the Norwich University campus. In this location it serves as a monumental anchor for the lower campus to the south. The site, chosen by the architect in concert with the Board of Trustees, was transformed from a parking lot into a large circle of grass and native plantings, patterned by walks and a new access road.

The building's mass, which contains approximately 50,000 square feet above ground and 8,000 square feet below, is broken into a main, six-story block surrounded by four discreet pavilions that conceal intake and exhaust facilities for the HVAC equipment. Cornice and roof lines of the main building align with existing university structures adjoining the site, while the pavilions are scaled to

the smaller, residential, utility, and commercial structures to the east and north of the library.

The library's architectural character is based on traditional Vermont prototypes in massing, style, and materials. Monumental civic and institutional buildings of Vermont from the Federalist, Greek Revival, and Colonial Revival periods were commonly timber-framed structures with clapboard exteriors, double- or triple-hung windows, and tall hipped or gabled roofs sheathed in metal or slate. The library attempts to reflect this language in a contemporary way, with its white clapboard siding on a Vermont granite base, wood windows, and a standing seam copper roof, crowned with dormers and a central chimney cluster.

Above: *The lower-scaled buildings adjacent to the library are on axis with pedestrian pathways. At night, the illuminated library becomes a beacon on the campus.*
Photo: Richard Mandelkorn

Right: *The mezzanine level overlooking the lobby undulates around a corner of the space.*
Photo: Richard Mandelkorn

CATION
THAT SHALL
BE AMERICAN IN ITS CHARACTER TO ENABLE THEM TO ACT AS
W
Reference

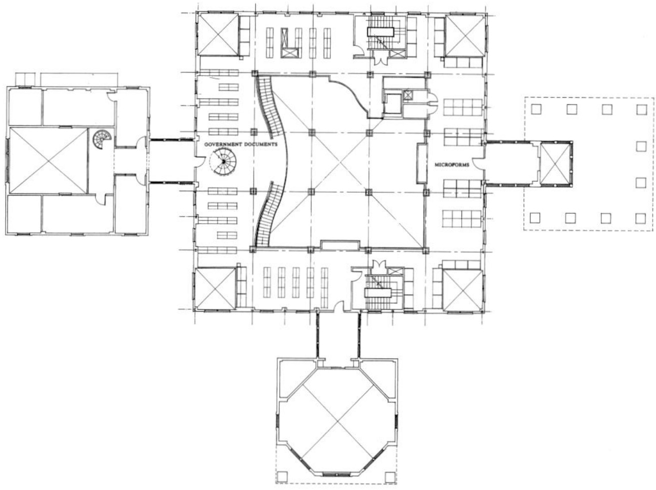

BALCONY FLOOR PLAN

FIRST FLOOR PLAN

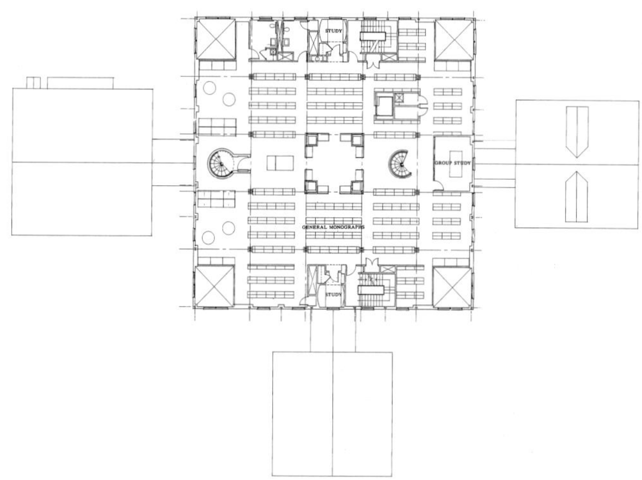

THIRD FLOOR PLAN

Left: *Spiral staircases throughout the library, such as this one on the third floor, permit quick circulation between levels.*
Photo: Richard Mandelkorn

Overleaf: *The first-floor entry features, to the right, a reception desk, and a double curved staircase leading to the Government Documents collection.*
Photo: Richard Mandelkorn

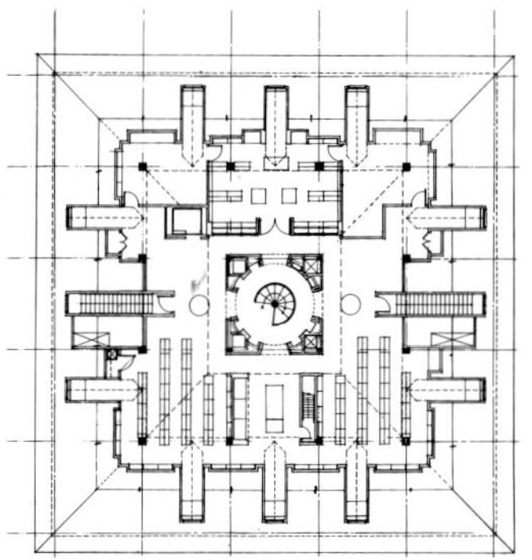

ATTIC FLOOR PLAN

1st Floor

THE NEW ENGLAND EXECUTIVE OFFICES

The 10,000-square-foot executive floor of the New England Life Insurance Company's headquarters was in nearly its original configuration, when the company decided to expand. The expansion project required modifications to the existing layout and space size without changing the original character of the board room and the board dining room. Design restraints included the need to execute construction without interrupting business during working hours, thus requiring a phasing plan.

Among the program elements of this interior design project is a state-of-the-art audio/visual-equipped conference room with many concealed features including a retractable video projector in the ceiling and computerized controls

recessed in the top of the conference table. Dark woods are used throughout the design to contrast with bright colors selected for furnishings, and light walls.

Overall, the project's crisp, Modern lines, simple detailing, and restrained color palette, bear a strong kinship to Japanese and Shaker design styles. The resulting atmosphere of subdued beauty reinforces the company's image of solid, affordable reliability.

Above: *The interior contrasts dark woodwork with light walls and colorful furnishings.*
Photo: Richard Mandelkorn

Right: *Built-in storage is crisply detailed to communicate a sense of refinement. Detailing throughout evokes the simplicity and solidity of Shaker design.*
Photo: Richard Mandelkorn

NORTH SHORE COMMUNITY COLLEGE

North Shore Community College urgently needed multi-purpose instructional space because of its diverse programs and growing student enrollment. A local business stepped forward and donated an empty industrial building to the State to meet the needs of the college. When state funding for renovating the building was not forthcoming, the college joined an association of schools in applying for Federal funds, which helped support a phased construction program.

After studying the 51,000-square-foot metal building shell, a strategy was developed to insert a partial second floor in a double-height space, adding an additional 29,000 square feet. Because of the college's rural location, the building has been designed to be self-contained, providing all necessary education

and student services on-site. The expanded facility is divided into three zones: classrooms, a student union, and administrative offices.

The educational program is devoted to the pure sciences and the preparation for careers in the Allied Health professions. Eight specialized classrooms, each with an adjoining laboratory, support these functions. Two lecture halls—a tiered, 110-seat hall and an 80-seat hall that can be partitioned into two 40-seat rooms—are also included.

The student services area includes a 350-seat cafeteria, a bookstore and a series of lounges for study and relaxation. Major arcades on each floor emphasize a "street vocabulary" that unifies the zone: passersby can peer into each area through storefront windows. Pedestrian benches dot the length of the arcade in streetscape fashion.

Large monitors with grids of skylights allow natural light to pour into the cafeteria and main student lobby, increasing the floor to ceiling height and creating an atmosphere of expansiveness. All senior administration officers and their support staff are located in an area which also contains a board room. Faculty offices are placed adjacent to the teaching area.

Above: *The student lounge on the second floor overlooks the cafeteria and a dramatically sloping glazed wall.*
Photo: Brian Vanden Brink

Right: *At the heart of the building, a new glass wall was added to deliver natural light to the area.*
Photo: Brian Vanden Brink

Above: *Classrooms are entered under a loggia, with a campus bookstore adjacent.*
Photo: Brian Vauden Brink

FIRST FLOOR PLAN

Above: *A quirky, curved staircase is wide and inviting to accommodate the building's population of students and faculty.*
Photo: Brian Vanden Brink

Overleaf: *The cafeteria is a sunny oasis for relaxation and socializing.*
Photo: Brian Vanden Brink

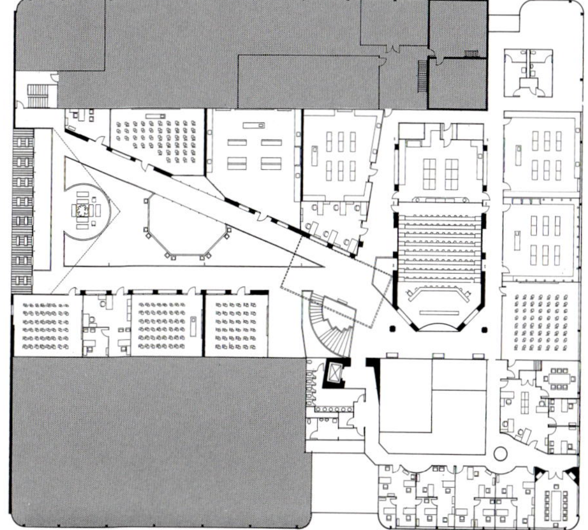

SECOND FLOOR PLAN

McKINSEY & COMPANY OFFICES

The new address for McKinsey & Company, an international management consulting firm, is a statement in itself. The Heritage on the Garden overlooks Boston's historic Public Garden and offers enviable views of the formal gardens and weeping willows surrounding a lagoon where the famous Boston Swan Boats glide throughout the summer.

A major goal in the design of this 23,300-square-foot office interior was to maintain views of the Public Garden and to share as much natural light as possible. The new layout is organized with emphasis on the public spaces. The perimeter offices of executives and managers rely on the dramatic backdrop of the garden for visual impact. The inner spaces also have views to the outside by

uniformly incorporating painted French doors with sidelights into all enclosed offices.

Visitors enter the main door and are oriented to a north-south axis down a long corridor that ultimately reveals a view of the Public Garden. The outer portion of the office is devoted to client space, including three conference rooms with mullioned glass walls, door casings, and millwork trim of a Georgian character and proportion.

The reception area features a custom reception desk of stained mahogany with cherry inserts and a polished granite top. The warm cherry floor is in gold tones, laid out in a herringbone pattern with a custom inlay compass and border accent of walnut and purpleheart.

Work areas are organized in a repetitive pattern of executive perimeter offices and interior associate offices served by secretarial stations arranged in a pod manner. An employee kitchen/dining room is playfully decorated in a muted gray and yellow color scheme with red accents.

Above: *A lounge area connecting to a reception space features a cherry floor in a herringbone pattern, with a walnut and purpleheart border.*
Photo: Richard Mandelkorn

Right: *The plush blue carpeting in the reception area corresponds to the fabric selections of burgundy and violet with gold highlights.*
Photo: Richard Mandelkorn

UNITED STATES EMBASSY

This 200,000-square-foot complex is situated on a 13-acre site and includes a chancery office building, chancery annex, ambassador's residence, Marine guard quarters, and an American Club, as well as a warehouse and motor pool. One of the first embassies to be built after the terrorist bombing in Beirut, the complex incorporates full State Department security measures including a high perimeter wall, deep building setbacks, sallyport entrances, and small windows and doors.

The design of the compound emphasizes the simple geometric forms, stone detailing, and landscaping that characterize the architectural vocabulary of the region while providing for the emblematic, programmatic, and security requirements of an embassy. Jordanian stone is used throughout the compound.

Buildings are primarily white stone with orange, yellow, green, and black stone used as accent and decoration. Gardens and pergolas, created as special enclosed green spaces, tie together the white stone forms of the buildings.

The interior design also affirms the architectural traditions of the local context. The boldness and massiveness of Middle Eastern building forms, with their large masonry units are counterbalanced by the traditional fine-detailing of wrought iron grillwork and wonderfully intricate mosaics. Also, the bright colors of the mosaics enliven the bold architectural forms with an interplay of light and dark colors. The interiors of the embassy blend elements of bold Middle Eastern color and scale with a sense of North American traditionalism. Bold forms for furniture, and upholstery with bright colors are designed to represent the United States' "patchwork" heritage.

Above: *The entry to the embassy complex features native stone with accents of bright color.*
Photo: Richard Mandelkorn

Right: *The yellow stucco wall of the chancery courtyard is punctuated with rusticated stone and bright red window grilles.*
Photo: Richard Mandelkorn

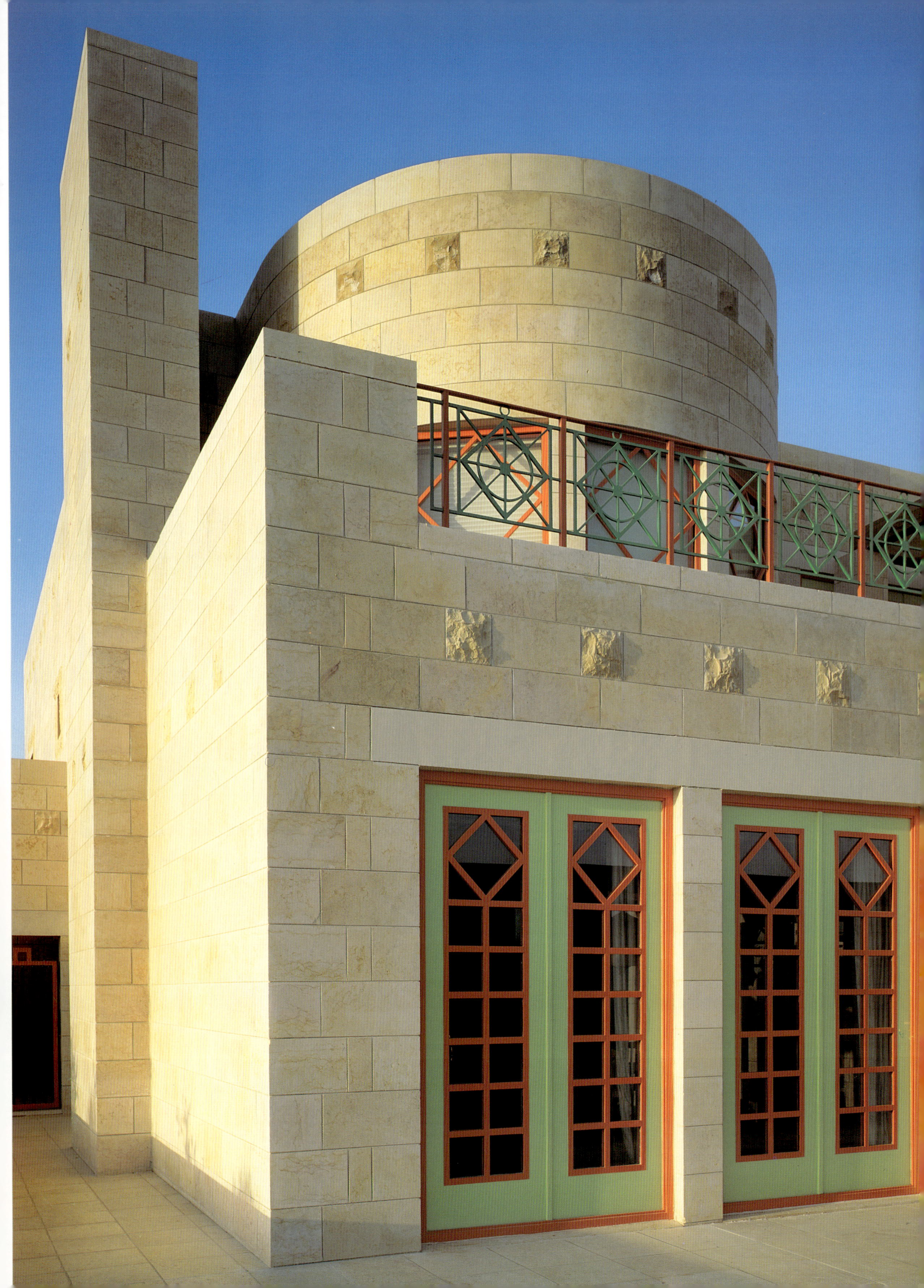

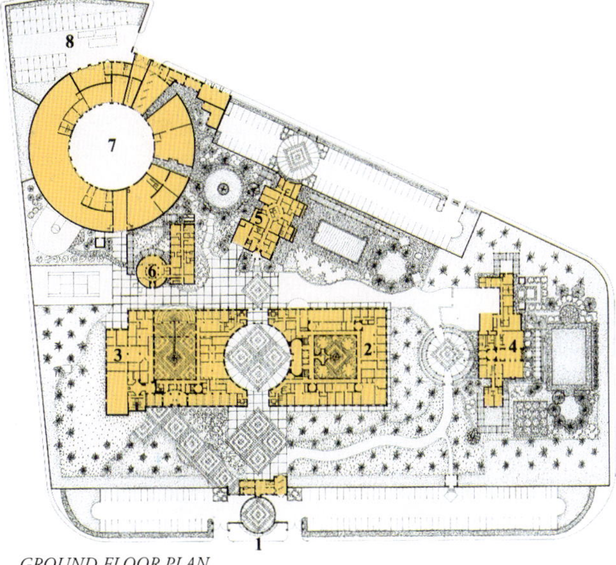

Above: *The north facade of the ambassador's residence is crowned with cube and cylinder forms.*
Photo: Richard Mandelkorn

Left: *The northeast corner of the building is distinguished by simple forms and bright colors.*
Photo: Richard Mandelkorn

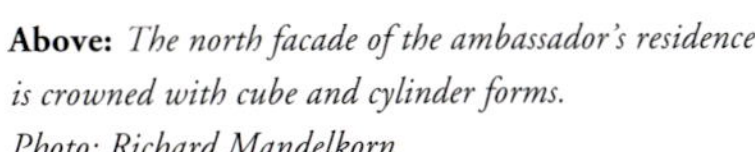

GROUND FLOOR PLAN

Above: *The motor court of the ambassador's residence features a trellis for shade in the desert climate.*
Photo: Richard Mandelkorn

Below: *The entry to the Marine guard quarters uses smooth and rusticated stone in light and dark tones.*
Photo: Richard Mandelkorn

Left: *The interior court of the chancery is marked with a bright yellow wall that contrasts with the desert's deep blue sky.*
Photo: Richard Mandelkorn

Opposite Page: *The view north from the second-floor balcony of the American Club overlooks the pool.*
Photo: Richard Mandelkorn

Overleaf Photo: Richard Mandelkorn

LIBRARY RESOURCE CENTER

RICHARD W. RILEY HALL

Richard W. Riley Hall on the Furman University campus houses the math and computer science departmental offices, classrooms, lounges, and a computer center in approximately 35,000 square feet on two levels. The entire Furman campus, since its inception in the early 1950s, has been designed by Perry Dean Rogers & Partners. The math and computer science building, executed in the stylized neo-Georgian vernacular of the campus, incorporates state-of-the-art systems and technology in the classrooms and computer center. These rooms include a small "theater" with tiered, built-in computer tables and a flexible array

of audio visual aids; several classrooms with raised access flooring; and a Learning Resource Center where students are able to work independently with the various computer systems and software in which they are receiving instruction.

The building takes the form of a long brick bar, similar to other buildings on the Furman campus. Its gabled roof is crowned with light monitors and ventilation stacks, which reinforce its neo-Georgian character and prepare one for the brightly colored lightwells inside. Under three of these roof-top monitors are open wells through the second floor to ground level, which bring natural light deep into the building and allow the inhabitants to track the path of the sun over the course of the day. Intense colors, as many as 16 in one room, are used throughout the space to distinguish various departmental areas, and to enliven long corridors.

Above: *The exterior of Richard W. Riley Hall is sympathetic to the neo-Georgian architecture of the Furman campus.*
Photo: Richard Mandelkorn

Opposite Page: (top) *A cone-shaped monitor brings in natural light and also allows views into the space from the corridor.*
Photo: Richard Mandelkorn
(center) *Natural light is brought into central corridors through skylights and is delivered to the lower level via open wells.*
Photo: Richard Mandelkorn
(bottom) *Even stairwells are ablaze with hot colors, such as pink, aqua blue, and purple, to contrast with muted tile walls.*
Photo: Richard Mandelkorn

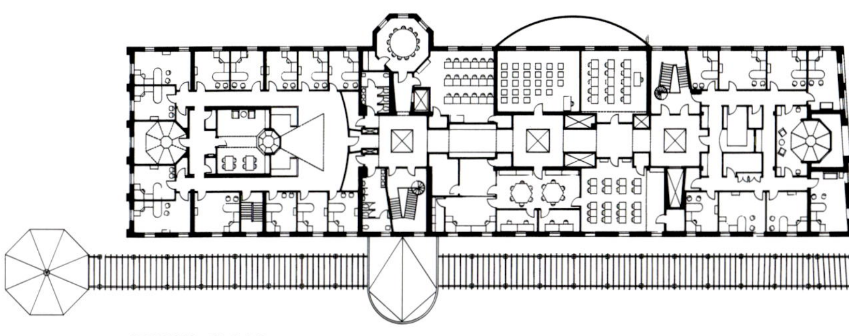

SECOND FLOOR

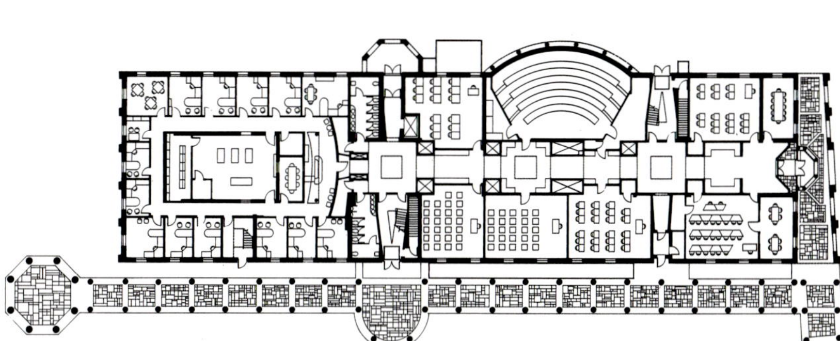
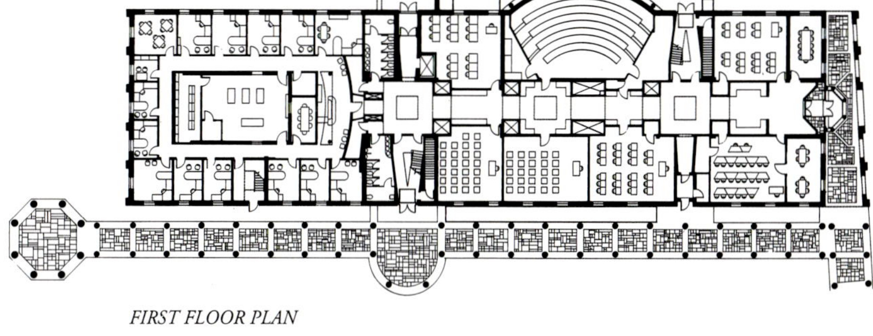

FIRST FLOOR PLAN

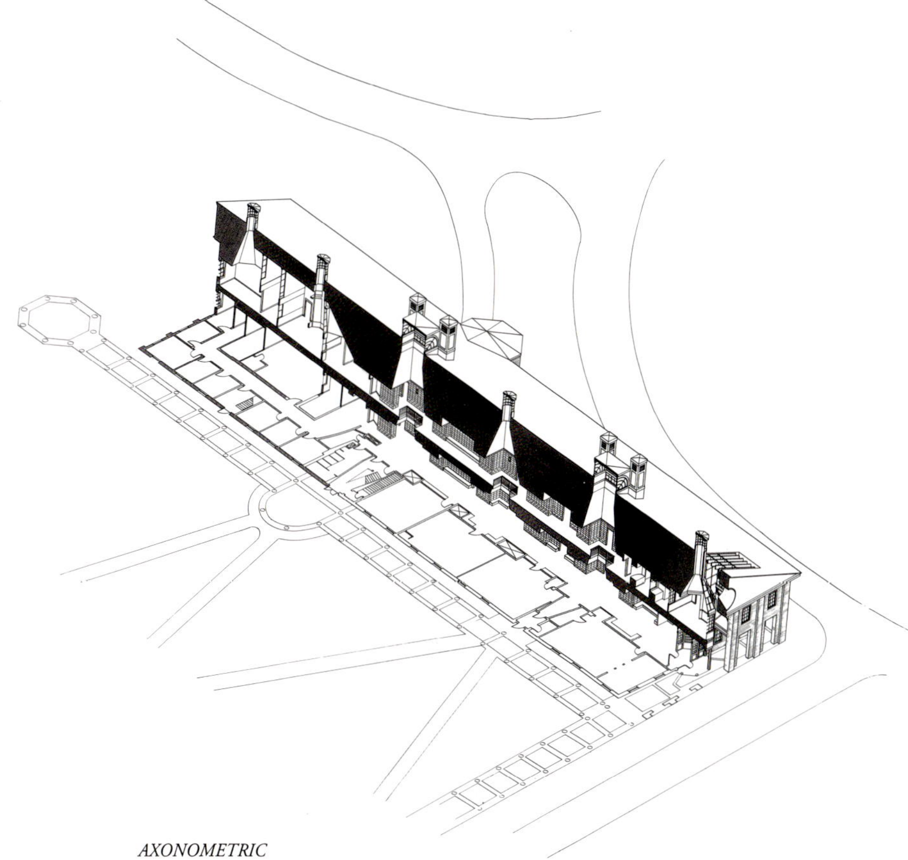

AXONOMETRIC

DORMITORIES AND
DINING HALL

Built on a previously swampy site, this dormitory and dining hall complex creates a new focus for the lower campus of Boston College. Two new dormitories, together housing 734, and a dining hall seating 930, are arranged around open space intended as an urban plaza.

The dormitories offer housing for students previously lodged off-campus, thus providing a more secure setting for student life. The dorms are divided into suites, ranging in size from four to eight beds. The six-story dormitory blocks are Modern in appearance, at the client's request—in deliberate contrast to the Collegiate Gothic building of the main campus. The dormitories define the north and east sides of the open plaza and are rendered in simple, buff-colored

brick. The plaza itself is paved with two shades of gray concrete pavers in a bold pattern. At the ends of the bar-like dormitories are glazed prows, which terminate the buildings.

The dining hall, situated on the site's south side, is entered through a cube-like port-cochere which is oriented toward pedestrian traffic from the north, east, and west. The dining hall's north elevation mimics an arcade with its repetition of structural bays with bay windows above. The exposed roof structure and stone hearth in the two-story main dining room are reminiscent of early collegiate dining halls.

Above: *The entry portico of the dining hall is designed
as a glazed cube sitting on a brick base.
Photo: Richard Mandelkorn*

Right: *The tower of the north dorm marks an entrance into the
housing block and gives the building an urban scale.
Photo: Richard Mandelkorn*

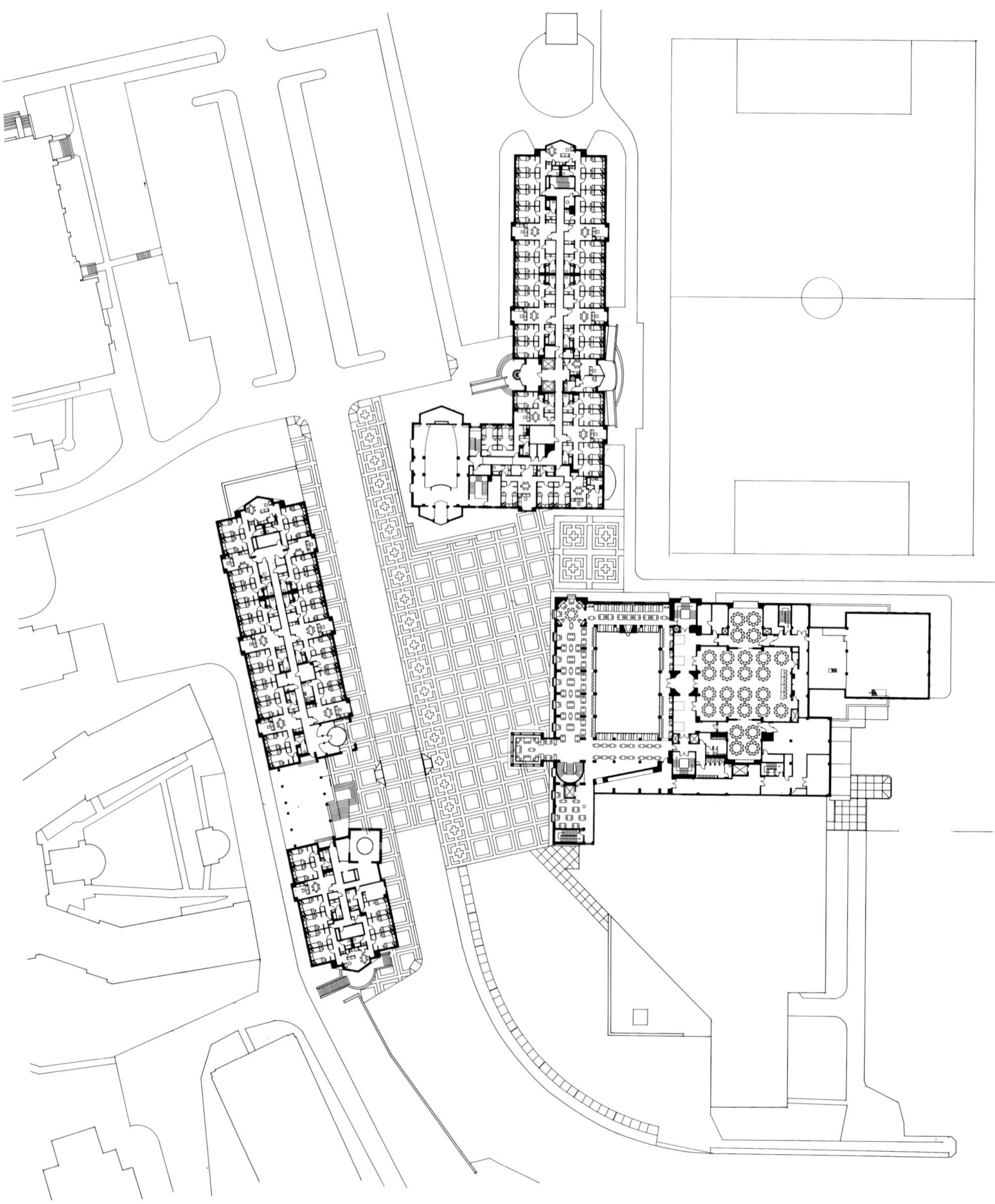

SITE PLAN

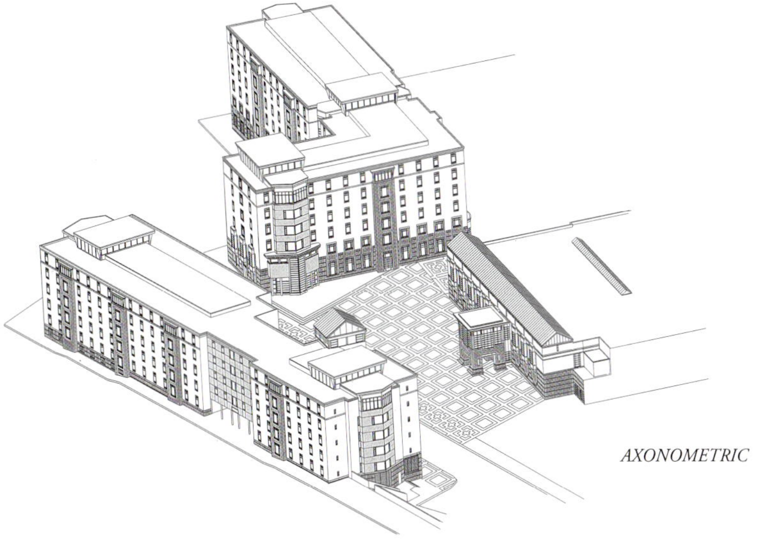

AXONOMETRIC

Above: *The connecting wall of the north dorm is rendered in scored stucco, recalling the paving design of the plaza while its tower gives the scale of an Italian piazza.*
Photo: Richard Mandelkorn

CUNY LIBRARY

The Library and Student Center for the CUNY/Staten Island is a joint design effort of Perry Dean Rogers & Partners and Mayers & Schiff, each of which developed one building after collaboration on the conceptual design. The buildings are organized along the primary campus axis and define the centers of the north and south academic quadrangles. They are conceptually related in parti massing and choice of materials, while the diverse nature of the respective programs is expressed in the different formal approaches to the plan; the Library maintains a classical stance against the dynamic, fluid aspects of the Student Center, which heightens the tension between the structures. The Library and Student Center are joined by an alley that is visually terminated to the south by the Library and to the north by the Student Center.

The Library is a square three-story structure with a central rotunda into which is inserted a large, octagonal screen. Entry is from the north through a smaller rotunda made of glass block and flanked with a glazed curtain wall. At the south side of the building is a large double-height reading room, which terminates the main campus axis.

The rotunda is naturally lit through clerestory windows behind the octagonal screen, and with artificial light sources, one of which illuminates the glass block lantern, and echoes an identical structure at the peak of the Student Center. These beacons define the campus center. The roof structure in this central space is entirely exposed, and the play of light and shadow among the network of trusses, rafters, and cables give this room its dramatic dimension.

Primary library user functions, such as reference, circulation, periodicals, and collection catalogue, are adjacent to the central rotunda on the first and second floors, while the top floor houses the bulk of the collection. On the second floor, a large balcony containing the periodicals collection overlooks the double-height reference room. Small skylit studies define a raised central area around the rotunda on the third floor. The glazed, open corners on this level provide oases for readers among the expanse of the stacks.

Above: *Metal and glass articulate the corners of the library and give them definition.*
Photo: Paul Warchol

Right: *Color is used to add interest in the library's major public spaces.*
Photo: Paul Warchol

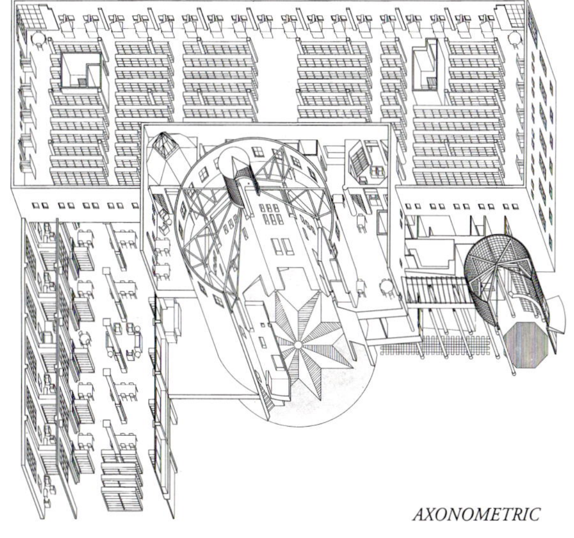

AXONOMETRIC

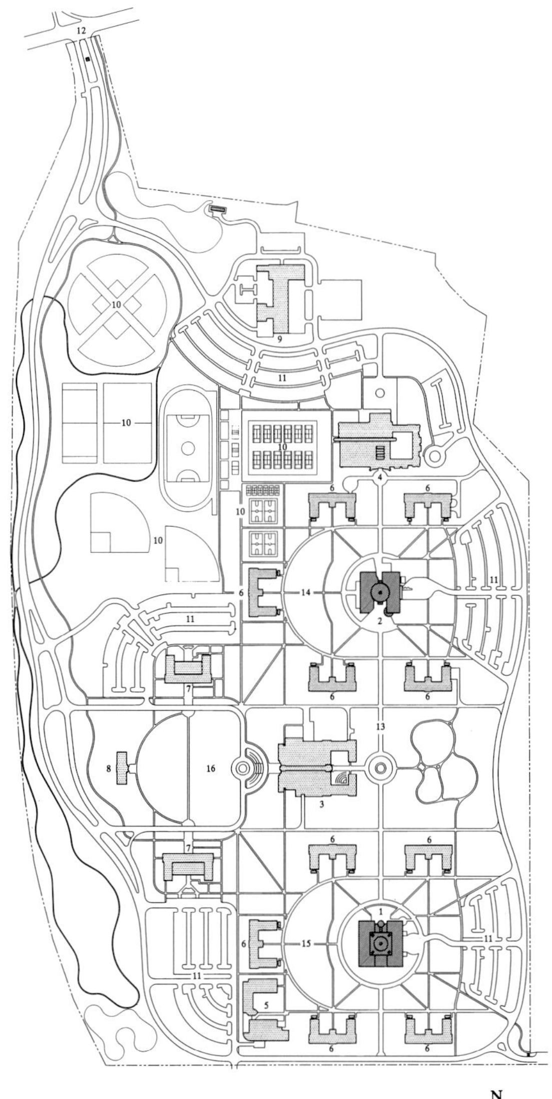

1 Library
2 Student Center
3 Performing Arts Center
4 Gymnasium
5 Laboratory Buildings
6 Academic Buildings
7 Administration
8 Visitor Center
9 Maintenance & Central Plant
10 Athletic Fields
11 Parking
12 Main Campus Entrance
13 Student Walk
14 North Academic Quadrangle
15 South Academic Quadrangle
16 The Lawn

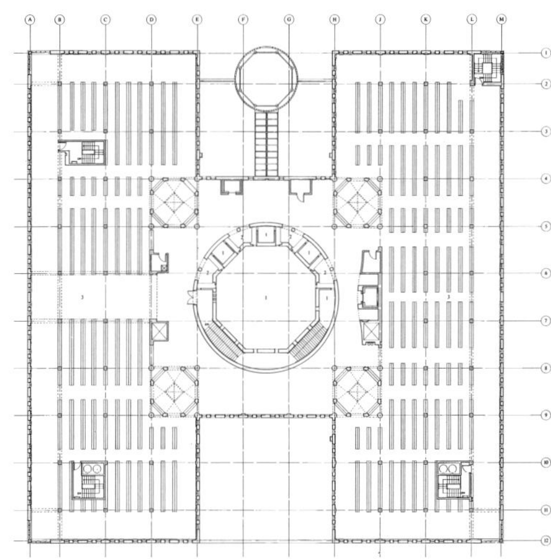

THIRD FLOOR PLAN

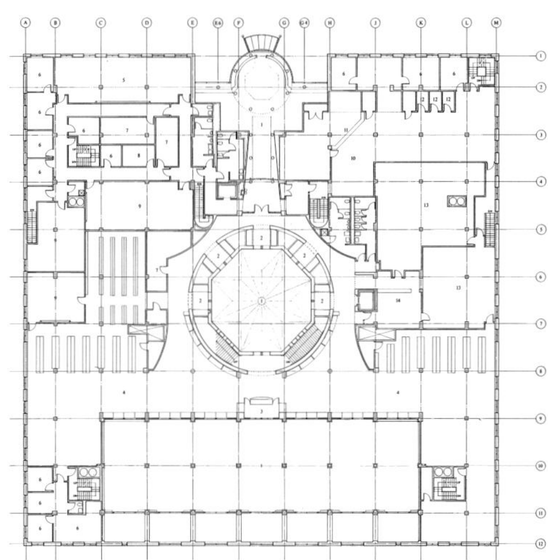

SECOND FLOOR PLAN

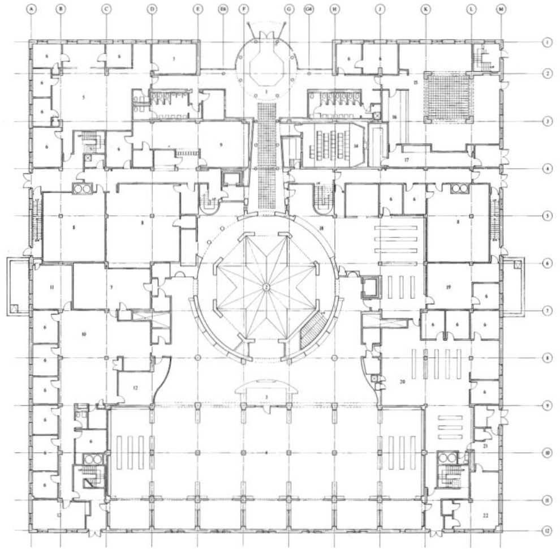

GROUND FLOOR PLAN

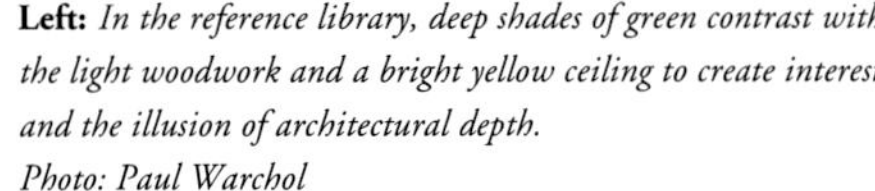

Left: *In the reference library, deep shades of green contrast with the light woodwork and a bright yellow ceiling to create interest and the illusion of architectural depth.*
Photo: Paul Warchol

Left: *The main rotunda space at the center of the library is surrounded by splayed openings that illuminate reading carrels, stairways, and circulation space.*
Photo: Paul Warchol

Below: *The glass-block entry lobby becomes a luminescent drum when viewed from outside.*
Photo: Paul Warchol

Right: *The roof the the rotunda space has an exposed steel structure and a glass-block cupola.*
Photo: Paul Warchol

Opposite Page: *A view through the entrance lobby, populated by a circle of steel columns with bright yellow capitals and red bases, reveals the Student Center in the distance, on axis with the library.*
Photo: Paul Warchol

Overleaf: *A pedestrian route with a fountain connects the library to the student center.*
Photo: Paul Warchol

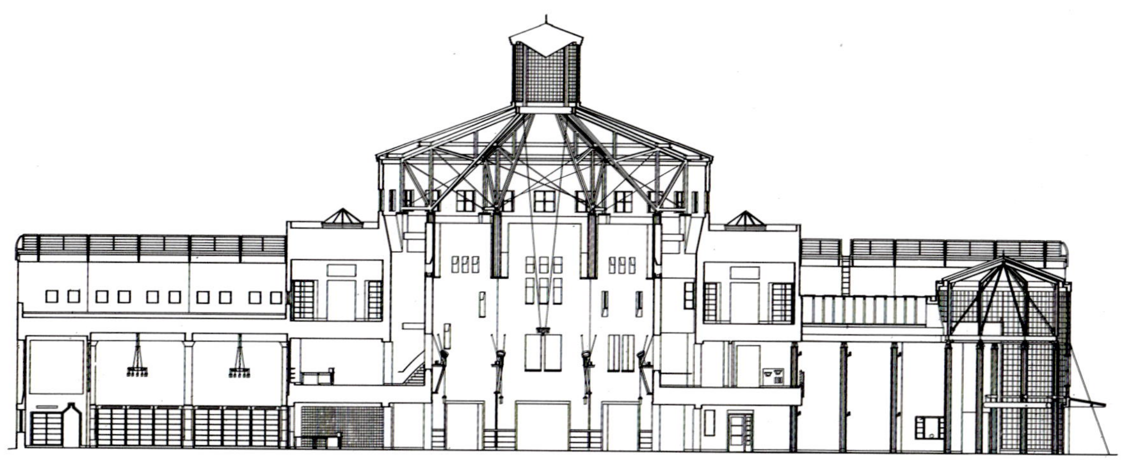

STUDENT ACTIVITIES
VILLAGE

The Student Activities Village bridges two campuses at Hamilton College: the original 19th Century campus, and the campus of Kirkland College, which merged with Hamilton in 1978. The Village occupies a pivotal site between the two, in a natural glen. An old, salt barn occupies the heart of the village from which new buildings stretch out to students approaching from Kirkland and Hamilton. The renovated barn is now the primary point of orientation for the students. It features a colorful, columnar rotunda and includes areas for study, relaxation, and informal dining.

East of the salt barn is a series of lounges and porches leading to the events barn. The two lounges provide quiet, intimate places more remote from the

main circulation route for study or small group meetings. An open porch looks onto an outdoor patio, while a glazed winter porch overlooks the glen. The events barn, a round structure with a mezzanine, is designed to accommodate diverse activities such as dances, poetry readings, lectures, and concerts.

To the west of the barn is the student common, where students can exchange information on bulletin boards, electronic and otherwise. A diner in the style of the stainless steel highway emporiums of the 1940s is next to the common. From this vantage point, students can observe the traffic on the foot bridge between the Kirkland and Hamilton campuses. A post office housed in an octagonal form completes the complex.

The Village complex derives its character from the existing barns and the agrarian architecture of upstate New York, with its exposed timber structure and tongue-and-groove wood surfaces on the interior. Clapboard exterior siding is painted yellow to match the existing barns, and trimmed in white. Overall, the buildings have the simple elegance and strength of Shaker architecture, and stand in graceful contrast to the college's informal and natural landscape.

Above: *The diner interior is alive with chrome surfaces, painted metal, bright colors, and generous sunlight.*
Photo: Richard Mandelkorn

Right: *The back of the diner wing is rendered in lead-coated copper, a material commonly used for barn roofs.*
Photo: Richard Mandelkorn

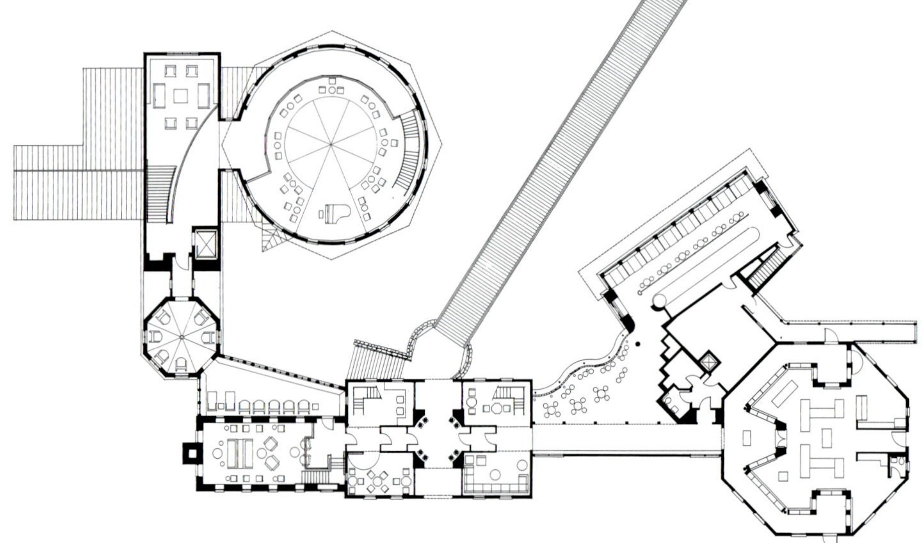

Above: *The circular events barn has a Shaker quality, and the exterior cladding provides a surface for the play of light.*
Photo: Richard Mandelkorn

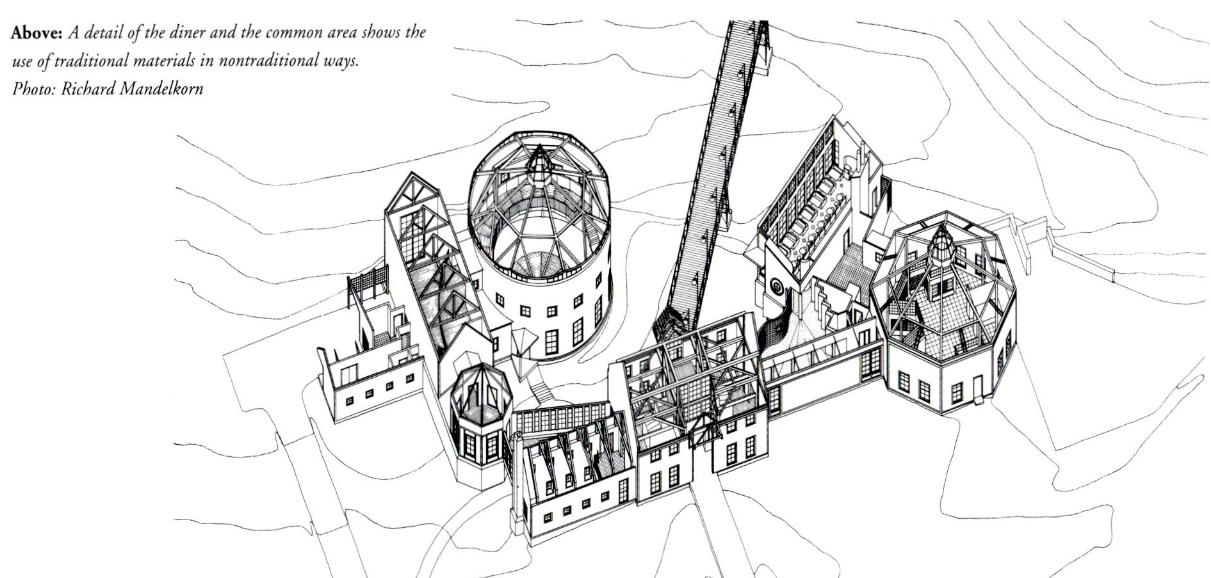

Above: *A detail of the diner and the common area shows the use of traditional materials in nontraditional ways.*
Photo: Richard Mandelkorn

Above: *Both bright and muted colors, applied to reveal the wood grain, are in keeping with the agrarian aesthetic.*
Photo: Richard Mandelkorn

Left: *The college post office is a double-height space contained within an octagonal form.*
Photo: Richard Mandelkorn

Below: *A detail of the events barn wall shows the use of mill-work inspired by decorative motifs common to farm buildings.*
Photo: Richard Mandelkorn

Opposite Page: *The lobby of the events barn allows quiet meeting places when the barn is not in use.*
Photo: Richard Mandelkorn

Overleaf: *The center, as approached from Kirkland campus, resembles a small village of agrarian buildings.*
Photo: Richard Mandelkorn

PERRY DEAN ROGERS
& PARTNERS

Principals
Robert C. Dean
(1992)
Steven M. Foote
Francis D. McGuire
Dell Mitchell
Martha A. Pilgreen
Peter A. Ringenbach
Charles F. Rogers

Senior Associates
David Fixler
Thomas McCarty
Donald Roche Jr.
Janet Stegman

Associates
Frank Chirico
Jeffrey Heyne
Bruce Hutt
Michael Sullivan
Joan Tommy
Paul Viccia

Collaborators
(1972-1995)
Lisa Abeles
Ann Abernathy
Frank Adams
Kishore Advani
Mary Ann Agresti
Patricia Albano
Charles Alexander
Abbot Allschwang
Shawn Alshut
Marty Anderson
Richard Anderson
Elsa Anguita
Christopher Anzuoni
Mary Applegate
John Atwood,
Darute Austras
Deborah Babson
Brian Back
Lynne Baldasare
Barbara Balluffi
Hannah Banks
Maureen Bannon
Alberta Baratelli
Bradley Barker
Alicia Bartlett
Joseph Behles
Patrick Belizaire
Joan Berg
John Berg
Juerg Bernet
Lee Beyer

Paul Bierman-Lytle
Wendy Blakeman
Trina Borning
Stephan Bosselman
Sarah Bourn
Darlene Brown
Eugene Brown
Arlene Brush
Peter Butler
Tanya Butler
Peter Byerly
James F. Cachelin
Robert Caddigan
Ralph Cadorette
Michael Cadwell
Margaret Callister
Blair Calvert
Constance Carell
David Carlson
Rachel Celeste
Henry Cerqua
Walter Chambers
Hingman Chan
Philip Chester
Benjamin Chirgwin
Chris Christodoulou
Roberta Ciarfella
Charles Clutz
Tami Cobbs
Tonia Coletti
Gerald Collette
George Collins
Marta Connolly
Edmund Cormier
Donald Corner
Susan Cory
Mark Cottle
Faith Cowgill
Irene Cowhig
Kathyanne Cowles
Charles Craig
Grace Cribbin
Deborah Cross
Jay Cross
Alicia Crowell
Fiske Crowell
Lisa Cullen
Scott Cullen
James Cullion
Julie Cunningham
Charles D'Avolio
Jesarielle Damora
Hope Dana
David Davies
Andrew J. Dean
Joseph DeAngelis
Debra DeLong

Gregory Dembs
Kim Denkewicz
Jeannine DeRoeck
Christine Desmond
Lowell Dewhirst
Rosanne Dicesare
Douglas Dick
Meliti Dikeos
Daniel Dilts
Charles Doherty
Robin Donhoff
Elizabeth Donnelly
Fred Dudu
Susan Dudzinski
Jane Duff
James Duffey
Stan Dunbar
Michael Duncan
Pamela Dunkle
Lloyd Dyson
Vicki Elms
Joann Engels
Elizabeth Ericson
Herbert Everett
Stephen Evers
Drayton Fair
Enrico Fanfani
Laurie Fanger
Charlene Faro
James Favaro
Stephanie Felch
David Feth
Hans Finne
Denise Finnegan
Michael Firkins
Dianne Fish
Jeffrey Fishbein
Conover Fitch Jr.
Margaret Fitzpatrick
Paula Fleck
Leo Fleming
William Fleming
Kelly Fogarty
Diane Forsstrom
Sarah Fortune
Abigail Frank
John Freeman
Ray Freeman
Jonathan Friend
Peter Furgiuele
Peter Gadsby
Daniel Gallagher
Kathleen Galvin
John Gardner
Vincent Gardner
Joanne Gasser
Rafael Gavilanes

Katherine Gehris
Gabriel Gelbart
Tancho Georgiev
Martha Gergely
Frederick Gibson
Sheila Gomes
Susan Greco
Collace Greene
Thomas Greene
Timothy Grobleski
Adam Gross
Peter Guzy
Arthur Hall
Cara Hall
Elbert Hall
Jeffrey Hall
Jonathan Halper
Stephen Hamilton
Deborah Handy
Christopher Hanlon
Robert Hannisian
Theresa Harriman
Elise Harris
Michael Harris
William Harris
Nancy Harrod
Elisabeth Hartman
John Hathaway
Pamela Hankins
James E. Heavey
Merville Hebert
Andrew Hepburn
Mary Lou Herlihy
Thomas Hess
Gavin Hilgemeier
Stephanie Hodal
Lorens Holm
Susan Holsclaw
Lynn Hopffgarten
Peter Hornbeck
Paul Hosey
Hiromi Hosoya
Chiway Hsiung
Jayne Hunter
Pegg Hunter
Walter Jacob
George Johnson
Marjorie Johnson
Susan Johnston
Carole Kassir
Carol Keller
Theresa Kelley
Mary Kenneally
Jane Kennedy
Chris Kilbridge
Jennifer King
Judith Kinnard

Lynne Klemmer
Michael Koehler
Nicholai Kolesnikoff
Jeanne Kopacz
Neil Kosak
Janet Kozun
David Krawitz
Michael Kubinski
Eben Kunz
Kathleen Kyle
Treffle LaFleche
Jean LaGuerre
Roger Lang
Anne Langton
Sandra Lanigan
Michael Lauber
David Laurin
Michael LeBlanc
Marjorie Lee
Carolyn Legg
Thomas Lemanski
William Lennertz
Mae Lesberg
Monica Letourneau
Barbara Lightfoot
William Lim
Shyun-kee Lin
Elizabeth Lindsley
Marleen Lipsick
Matthew Littell
George Lloyd
Neil Loden
Catherine Logue
Barbara Lorente
George Lovely
Nu-Nu Luan
Allan MacDonald
Joyce MacDonald
Sharon Mackenzie
Susan Mackey
Glenn MacWalter
Philip Madonia
Elizabeth Mahon
Hermes Mallea
Marjorie Marks
Robert Marks
Neil Martin
Kelly Mason
Peter Matthews
Richard Mauser
John McCarthy
Margaret McDonagh
Nancy McDonald
Michael McDonnell
James McHugh
Henry McInnis
Susan McLean

Ross McNamara
Glenn Mead
Robert Miklos
Wendy Mininberg
Clifford Minnick
Hitome Mochidome
Elinor Moore
David Morse
David Moser
Stephen Moser
David Mullen
Joseph Mulligan
David Mullman
Lynda Murry
John Napier
Gretchen Neeley
Margaret Nelson
Laura Newman
Doreve Nicholaeff
Tim Nissen
Eleanor Norris
Constance Nucci
Paul Nyquist
Kathleen O'Neil
George O'Neill
Michael Oldakowski
Charles Osborne
Donald Paine
Charles Parkhurst
Paul Patturelli
Gary Paul
Mary Paulson
Monte Payette
Allan Perry
Frederic Pierce
David Pimental
Ann Pitt
Edward Polk
Christopher Pollack
Lisa Popitz
Catherine Porzio
Elizabeth Porzio
Richard M. Potter
Heidi Princevalle
Doreen Puccini
Thomas Queenan
Patrick Quinlan
Charles Quinn
Frederick Read
Ann Reed
Lisa Reindorf
Jennifer Remedios
Bruce Rhoades
Mia Ricci
Daphne Rice
Jeanne Rice
Ronald Richer

Ana Rico-Perez
Polly Ringenbach
Robert Rink
Virginia Rinn
Meredith Robbins
Kenneth Roberts
David Robinson
Donald Roche
Robert Roche
Barbara Rodi
Francesca Rogier
Karen Rosenberg
Tatiana Ruzicka
Stephen Ryan
John Ryder
Cynthia Sallee
Luis Saltiel
Judith Salvi
Kenneth Savoie
Richard Sawler
John Scaramuzzo
Debin Schliesman
Erika Schroeder
John Schuyler
Alan Schwabenland
Richard Schwartz
Neal Schwartz
Paul Scott
Stanley S. Setchell
Wendy Shapiro
Gary Shaw
Thomas Shaw
Roger Sherman
Steven Shoreman
Jeannette Shriver
Helen Sides
Sam Silipo
Marlayna Silva
Marshall Silva
Michael Sinesi
Richard Smith
Ross Smith
Julia Smyth
Ronda Snyder
Michael Soucy
Francis St. Pierre
Frederick Stahl
Susan Steele
Glen Steer
Laurie Stevenson
Judith Stewart
David Storeyguard
James Styrsky
Gertrude Sullivan
Martha Sullivan
Patricia Sullivan
Catherine Suttle

David Suvak
Norman Swiatek
Austin Tang
Kathleen Tansey
Donald Taylor
Donald Tellalian
Richard Terrell
Laura Thomas
Roxi Thoren
Thomas Tidlund
Joseph Tomasello
Elaine Topousis
Paul Trapani
George Trembley
Allen Trousdale
Peter Tulupman
William Turville
Claire Twomey
Robert Upton
Kenneth Vais
Warren Van Wees
James Vaughan
Scott Vaughn
Sergio Verrillo
Robert Vigeant
Bradley Wales
Peter Wallis
Carol Walsh
Martin Wander
Barbara Ann Ward
Robert Ward
Val Warke
Michael Waters
Ellen Watts
Tobin Weaver
John Weil
Amy Weinstock
David Weisman
Sarah Wentworth
Erika White
Sara Whitten
Michael Williams
Timothy Wilson
Mark A. Wilterding
Renee Windward
Wayne Winslow
Janine Wong
Koonshing Wong
Liliane Wong
Charles Wood
Elise Woodward
Anna Wu
Gabriel Yaari
Jenny Young
Homa Zartoshty
Gregory Zorzi

*A*uthor's Note

Michael J. Crosbie, a senior editor of *Progressive Architecture,* author of several books on architecture, and the architecture critic for *The Hartford Courant,* is also a licensed architect. His articles have appeared in a variety of publications, including *Architecture, Fine Homebuilding, Historic Preservation,* and *Domus.* He teaches at Roger Williams University's School of Architecture, and lives with his family in Essex, Connecticut.